Docker Quick Start Guide

Learn Docker like a boss, and finally own your applications

Earl Waud

BIRMINGHAM - MUMBAI

Docker Quick Start Guide

Copyright © 2018 Packt Publishing

Commissioning Editor: Vijin Boricha
Acquisition Editor: Noyonika Das
Content Development Editor: Kirk Dsouza
Technical Editor: Niral Almeida
Copy Editor: Safis Editing
Project Coordinator: Hardik Bhinde
Proofreader: Safis Editing
Indexer: Tejal Daruwale Soni
Graphics: Alishon Mendonsa
Production Coordinator: Arvindkumar Gupta

First published: November 2018

Production reference: 1281118

Published by Packt Publishing Ltd.
Livery Place
35 Livery Street
Birmingham
B3 2PB, UK.

ISBN 978-1-78934-732-6

www.packtpub.com

Creating this book was a major undertaking and, as a result, I owe a debt of gratitude to many.

First, thank you to my Heavenly Father. Thank you for my days, and for my many blessings. Thank you for this book. Thank you for the opportunity to learn and grow as I created its content. Thank you for allowing me to get it right. And thank you for blessing all who read it so that they can find the solutions they need. I love Thee very much. Thank you.

Thank you to my amazing wife, Patti. Thank you, honey, for your patience with me and for being okay with all the time I had to invest in creating this book. You offered me unswerving support so that I could research, write, and revise the information within these pages and, without your support, this book would not exist. Thank you for your confidence in me. And thank you for loving me. Thank you for seeing me as your warrior king. Thank you for Finlee. I love you very much. Thank you.

Thank you to my daughter, Madison. Thank you, Madison, for your light, and for your faith in me. Thank you for seeing me the way that you do. I love you very much. Thank you.

Thank you to my daughter, Alexis. Thank you, Lexi, for believing in me. And thank you for the confidence and pride you have for me. Thank you for having faith in my ability to be a writer. I love you very much. Thank you.

Thank you to my daughter, Daniella. Thank you, Dani, for your energy and unique perspective. Thank you for your support and your belief in me and in my ability to write this book. I love you very much. Thank you.

Thank you to my friends and reviewers – Rod Foster, Jitesh Marathe, and Mert Cubukcuoglu. Thank you all for poring over the chapters of this book and making sure I've presented the most accurate content and examples possible. Thank you.

Thank you to my friend Tom "Big Al" Schreiter. Thank you, Tom, for suggesting that I start writing books and for being such a great example by taking your own advice and creating a fantastic set of training books. Thank you.

– Earl Waud

"I can no other answer make, but, thanks, and thanks."

– William Shakespeare

`mapt.io`

Mapt is an online digital library that gives you full access to over 5,000 books and videos, as well as industry leading tools to help you plan your personal development and advance your career. For more information, please visit our website.

Why subscribe?

- Spend less time learning and more time coding with practical eBooks and Videos from over 4,000 industry professionals

- Improve your learning with Skill Plans built especially for you

- Get a free eBook or video every month

- Mapt is fully searchable

- Copy and paste, print, and bookmark content

Packt.com

Did you know that Packt offers eBook versions of every book published, with PDF and ePub files available? You can upgrade to the eBook version at `www.packt.com` and as a print book customer, you are entitled to a discount on the eBook copy. Get in touch with us at `customercare@packtpub.com` for more details.

At `www.packt.com`, you can also read a collection of free technical articles, sign up for a range of free newsletters, and receive exclusive discounts and offers on Packt books and eBooks.

Foreword

By eliminating variability in shipping and logistics, containers revolutionized the world back in 1956. This paradigm shift alone increased trade between nations, grew markets to a global scale, and decreased loading costs by approximately 97%. Today, Docker containers are having a similar revolutionary impact on the IT industry that no one can afford to fall behind.

I have been in the industry for more than 14 years, leading next-generation technology implementation efforts in world-class enterprise companies where technology is in the heart of the business, contributing toward their revenue. Throughout my professional journey, I've had a chance to be a part of many technology shifts, including virtualization, public cloud, software-defined data centers, infrastructure as a code, and containers. Lately, I've been focusing on delivering a universal container image and artifact management platform for one of the top global fintech companies, Intuit.

I met the author of this book, Earl Waud, during a technology presentation back in 2010. First impressions matter most, and I accidentally spilled a cup of coffee on his notebook—which turned out to be the beginning of a lifelong friendship.

After knowing Earl for more than eight years, I would describe him as a very professional, innovative, methodical, self-driven, and genuine person, allowing him to achieve any goal that he desires. There are countless examples of him coming up with an innovative idea, designing it on paper, engineering it in the lab, and implementing it in production to help and serve mission-critical, multibillion-dollar, revenue-generating products.

Historically, the infrastructure side and the software side of the IT industry have been disconnected for a long time. There are many interdependencies between both sides, yet most of the technologies and capabilities were siloed and handled differently. Docker container technology is bridging this gap by introducing a standardized way of building, packaging, and delivering software. Although there are several container technologies available, many professionals have chosen to use Docker because it is one of the most stable and effective platforms.

In *Docker Quick Start Guide*, by Earl Waud, Earl clearly depicts how you can build, package, and deploy your software as a container. He provides insight into many container related technologies with hands-on examples, allowing you to pick the right containerization approach for your software. With the skill set that you will gain from this book, you will be able to transform your traditional software to containerized software very rapidly, effectively, and successfully for all your business needs.

If decreasing cost, time to market, and variability is important for your business, and software containerization is in your roadmap to achieve these goals, *Docker Quick Start Guide* is one of the most important references that you can have in your library.

I would like to conclude by, one more time, saying thank you to the author of this book, Earl Waud, for leading the way by setting an example for the rest of the world, both at a professional level and a personal level. *"We always win"* my friend.

– Mert Cubukcuoglu

Senior Manager, Intuit Inc.

Contributors

About the author

Earl Waud is a virtualization development professional with more than 20 year's experience developing customer-facing, enterprise-grade software for VM, and works with container provisioning, management, and automation.

Earl has a proven track record of delivering on-time solutions that significantly impact business results; solutions that align engineering strategies with organizational vision.

Recently, Earl has been creating AWS-based container solutions for enterprises using Docker, Kubernetes, Artifactory, Xray, and Twistlock.

Currently, Earl is a senior software engineer with Intuit Inc. Other books by Earl include *Mastering Chef Provisioning* and *Chef: Powerful Infrastructure Automation*. Earl can be found online at *SanDiegoEarl (dot) com*.

Thank you to the people without whom this book would not have been written. First, thanks to my Heavenly Father. Thanks also to my family: Patti, Alexis, Daniella, and Madison. Thanks to my friends and reviewers – Rod, Jitesh, and Mert. Thank you as well to my friend, Tom "Big Al" Schreiter. And finally, thanks to my entire Packt team, but especially Douglas Paterson, Kirk Dsouza, Hardik Bhinde, Noyonika Das, and Niral Almeida. Thank you all!

About the reviewers

Paul Adamson has worked as an Ops engineer, a developer, a DevOps engineer, and everything in between. When not reviewing this book, Paul keeps busy helping companies embrace the AWS infrastructure. His language of choice is PHP, for all the good reasons and even some of the bad, but mainly out of habit. While reviewing this book, Paul has been working for Healthy Performance Ltd, helping to apply cutting-edge technology to a cutting-edge approach to well being.

Mert Cubukcuoglu is a senior information technology leader with more than 12 years experience in implementing and leading enterprise-level, next-generation platform solutions within large data centers and the public cloud. His expertise in delivering mission-critical innovative technology solutions that are aligned with overall strategy and business goals provides him with a competitive advantage in any industry. Currently, Mert is leading compute engineering and automation teams at Intuit, a leader in the small business and personal finance software industry.

Rod Foster is an innovative, pro-active, and performance-driven Solutions Architect with more than 14 years of experience in the Information Technology and Services industry, including 10 years of direct focus on Virtualization. Rod is currently one of the leaders on Intuit's exceptional Cloud and Hypervisor Team, he is directly responsible for the engineering and implementation of Intuit's Cloud (AWS) and VMware vSphere architecture that support its TurboTax, QuickBooks, and Mint offerings. When Rod isn't busy innovating, mentoring and providing quality assurance oversight to Intuit's vast portfolio of services, he enjoys fitness, music, and traveling! Special thanks to Earl Waud for allowing me to take part in the creation of this book!

Jitesh Marathe is an IT professional with a Bachelor degree in Computer Application; he has spent most of his career being a System Administrator in various IT companies and specialized in the System and DevOps Role. Jitesh enjoys traveling to new places with his family. Jitesh has reviewed a few other books including *Linux Utilities Cookbook*, and *Mastering Linux Network Administration*.

Vishnu Gopal is an engineer with strong product and user-experience skills, with experience in product development, web development, and engineering management. He was part of the initial team that built SlideShare Inc., which then went on to be acquired by LinkedIn. He has been working in the web and mobile development field for over 10 years. He is currently CTO of SV.CO, a product accelerator for students based in India. He lives in Kochi, India.

I would like to thank Sanjay Vijayakumar, my best friend since school. In times happy and sad, in waters troubled and still, he's always been a constant soul in my life.

Packt is searching for authors like you

If you're interested in becoming an author for Packt, please visit `authors.packtpub.com` and apply today. We have worked with thousands of developers and tech professionals, just like you, to help them share their insight with the global tech community. You can make a general application, apply for a specific hot topic that we are recruiting an author for, or submit your own idea.

Table of Contents

Preface

Usually, the first question I get when I mention Docker or this book is *What is Docker?* So, we might as well answer that question right now and get it out of the way...

Within the circle of friends I hang out with, I would answer that question by saying *Docker is a software solution used to build, ship, and run containers anywhere.* But if you are not a computer person, then that answer would mean next to nothing to you. So, let's try again, and answer the question *What is Docker?* in a way that is worthy of a Quick Start Guide.

Docker is a tool that allows software developers to easily create applications, and wrap those applications in a special package called a **container**. Used correctly, an application packaged as a container can be run very efficiently, and very securely. And since the container has everything the application needs to run, it also allows the developer to share their application nearly anywhere, without ever having to re-create or re-package it.

This means that as a result of using Docker, a developer can create, run, and test their application container on their own laptop and then share the exact same container with their peers so that it can be run and tested by them as well. Then, they can share the same container with the quality assurance team for further validation of quality, and ultimately, the exact same container can be run and used by customers in a production setting.

Using Docker, software developers can create better, more secure software that can be tested and deployed faster than ever before.

Within the pages of this book, you are going to find all of the information that you need to understand what Docker is and what benefits Docker provides. Using detailed, yet easy-to-follow, descriptions and examples, this Quick Start Guide will teach you how to set up your own Docker development environment, and how to create enterprise-grade Docker images that utilize all of the important features that Docker provides. This Quick Start Guide will teach you how to use Docker networking and Docker's storage features. You will also learn how to create and deploy multi-container applications, and how to set up Docker clustering using Docker Swarm. By the time you finish the Quick Start Guide, you will be building and sharing your own Docker images, and running your most important applications in Docker containers. This Quick Start Guide will thoroughly prepare you to use Docker for all of your future projects. If you are ready to get started, turn the page...

Who this book is for

This Quick Start Guide is written for anyone who wants to know what Docker is and understand why so many people are so excited about using it. It is intended for developers who want to get started using Docker right away and don't have time to wade through a full *Mastering Docker* book, or attend a week-long training course. This guide is for anyone who needs to make a quick decision about using Docker for their next project and get started right away.

What this book covers

Chapter 1, *Setting up a Docker Development Environment*, covers getting everything set up for Docker development on our workstation. We learn how to set up a Docker development environment on Linux, Windows, and OS X workstations. We will then handle some post-installation steps for each OS. Lastly, we will learn how using Docker on each OS differs and what to watch out for between them.

Chapter 2, *Learning Docker Commands*, introduces a number of essential Docker commands. While we focus on one of the most important commands, the container run command, we will also cover many other commands that you will be using on a daily basis. These commands include the list container command, the stop container command, and the remove container command. Along the way, we will also discover other container commands, such as logs, inspect, stats, attach, exec, and commit. I think you will find this chapter to be an excellent foundation in terms of your Docker education.

Chapter 3, *Creating Docker Images*, covers how to create enterprise-grade Docker images. We will start off by learning about the main building block of Docker images; specifically, the Dockerfile. We will then explore all the instructions available to use in a Dockerfile. There are some instructions, that, on the face of it, will seem very similar. We will uncover the differences between the COPY and ADD instructions, the ENV and ARG instructions, and, most importantly, between the CMD and ENTRYPOINT instructions. Then, we will find out what the build context is and why it is important. Finally, we will cover the actual image build command.

Chapter 4, *Docker Volumes*, uncovers the secrets of Docker volumes. We will learn how to use folders on your workstation inside your Docker containers, as well as how to create and use persistent volumes, allowing multiple containers to share data. We will learn how to clean up after unused volumes. And finally, to round it out, we will learn how to create data volume containers to become the *source* of volumes for other containers.

Chapter 5, *Docker Swarm*, covers what Docker swarm is, and how to set up a Docker swarm cluster. We will find out more about swarm managers and swarm workers. We will discover Swarm Services. We will find out how easy it is to access a container application running on any node in the swarm cluster.

Chapter 6, *Docker Networking*, introduces Docker networking. We will dive deep into Docker networking, learning how containers can be isolated, how they can communicate with each other, and how they can communicate with the outside world. We will explore the local network drivers Docker provides in the out-of-the-box installation. We will then examine the use of remote network drivers with an example deployment of the Weave driver. After that, we will learn how to create Docker networks and round out the discussion with a look at the free services that we get with our Docker networks.

Chapter 7, *Docker Stacks*, brings together everything we will have learned in the first six chapters in order to be able to define, deploy, and manage multi-container applications. We will achieve this via the use of Docker stacks. We are going to learn how to use Docker stacks and the YAML files required to define multi-container applications. And, we will leverage what we learned about Docker services, Docker volumes, Docker swarm, and Docker networking to create full-featured, multi-service Docker-based applications.

Chapter 8, *Docker and Jenkins*, covers how to leverage Jenkins to build our Docker images and deploy our Docker containers. We will learn how to deploy our Jenkins server as a Docker container. We will follow that by learning how to build Docker images within the Dockerized Jenkins server. This is what is often referred to as *Docker in Docker*. Finally, we will see how to utilize Docker containers as the Jenkins build agents, allowing every build to be run in a pristine, ephemeral Docker container. Of course, we will show how to build Docker images, test applications, and push tested images to a Docker registry, all within our Dockerized Jenkins build agents. This will provide you with all the tools you will need to set up your CI/CD systems.

To get the most out of this book

You should have a developer workstation that you can install Docker on and use to test out the examples included in this book. You will learn the most by actually trying each of the examples yourself instead of just reading over them. In addition, you should have access to at least one other, but preferably two or three other, servers to configure as a Docker swarm. These servers can be EC2 instances in AWS; or VMs on VMware Workstation or Fusion; or, worst case scenario, VMs in VirtualBox. All of the software used throughout this book is free or open source, so you should be able to try out everything you are learning here. Most of the examples will work equally well regardless of the OS you are using, and I have tried to call out the differences where appropriate. You should have an account created on `https://hub.docker.com`, and an account on `https://github.com`. All of the code samples have been tested by me, as well as by several reviewers, so if you don't get them to work, double-check the code and try again, or download the code from Packt and cut and paste it into your system, and then try again. You'll get the hang of it.

Download the example code files

You can download the example code files for this book from your account at `www.packtpub.com`. If you purchased this book elsewhere, you can visit `www.packtpub.com/support` and register to have the files emailed directly to you.

You can download the code files by following these steps:

1. Log in or register at `www.packtpub.com`.
2. Select the **SUPPORT** tab.
3. Click on **Code Downloads & Errata**.
4. Enter the name of the book in the **Search** box and follow the onscreen instructions.

Once the file is downloaded, please make sure that you unzip or extract the folder using the latest version of:

- WinRAR/7-Zip for Windows
- Zipeg/iZip/UnRarX for Mac
- 7-Zip/PeaZip for Linux

The code bundle for the book is also hosted on GitHub at `https://github.com/PacktPublishing/Docker-Quick-Start-Guide`. In case there's an update to the code, it will be updated on the existing GitHub repository.

We also have other code bundles from our rich catalog of books and videos available at https://github.com/PacktPublishing/. Check them out!

Code in action

Visit the following link to check out videos of the code being run:
http://bit.ly/2Q1DbPq

Conventions used

There are a number of text conventions used throughout this book.

CodeInText: Indicates code words in text, database table names, folder names, filenames, file extensions, pathnames, dummy URLs, user input, and Twitter handles. Here is an example: "In the networks key section, we are instructing Docker to create two networks, one named frontend and one named backend."

Any command-line input or output is written as follows:

```
# Enable autolock on your swarm cluster
docker swarm update --autolock=true
# Adjust certificate expiry to 30 days
docker swarm update --cert-expiry 720h
```

Bold: Indicates a new term, an important word, or words that you see on screen. For example, words in menus or dialog boxes appear in the text like this. Here is an example: "Once the configuration has been saved, let's test the job by clicking on the **Build Now** link."

Warnings or important notes appear like this.

Tips and tricks appear like this.

Get in touch

Feedback from our readers is always welcome.

General feedback: Email feedback@packtpub.com and mention the book title in the subject of your message. If you have questions about any aspect of this book, please email us at questions@packtpub.com.

Errata: Although we have taken every care to ensure the accuracy of our content, mistakes do happen. If you have found a mistake in this book, we would be grateful if you would report this to us. Please visit www.packtpub.com/submit-errata, selecting your book, clicking on the Errata Submission Form link, and entering the details.

Piracy: If you come across any illegal copies of our works in any form on the internet, we would be grateful if you would provide us with the location address or website name. Please contact us at copyright@packtpub.com with a link to the material.

If you are interested in becoming an author: If there is a topic that you have expertise in, and you are interested in either writing or contributing to a book, please visit authors.packtpub.com.

Reviews

Please leave a review. Once you have read and used this book, why not leave a review on the site that you purchased it from? Potential readers can then see and use your unbiased opinion to make purchase decisions, we at Packt can understand what you think about our products, and our authors can see your feedback on their book. Thank you!

For more information about Packt, please visit packtpub.com.

Setting up a Docker Development Environment

"Suddenly it occurred to me: Would it not be great if my trailer could simply be lifted up and placed on the ship without its contents being touched?"

- Malcolm McLean, American trucking entrepreneur

In this chapter, we are going to get everything set up for Docker development on our workstation. We will learn how to set up a Docker development environment on Linux, Windows, and OS X workstations. Then we will handle some post-installation steps for each OS. Lastly, we will learn how using Docker on each OS differs and what to watch out for between them.

By the end of this chapter, you will know the following:

- How to set up your Docker development environment, irrespective of whether your workstation is running on the following:
    - CentOS
    - Ubuntu
    - Windows
    - OS X
- The differences to be aware of when using Docker on different OSes

Technical requirements

You will need a development workstation using the OS of your choice, including Linux, Windows, or OS X. You will need sudo or admin access on the workstation. And since you will be installing Docker software that will be pulled from the internet, you will need basic internet connectivity on your workstation.

The code files of this chapter can be found on GitHub:

```
https://github.com/PacktPublishing/Docker-Quick-Start-Guide/tree/master/
Chapter01
```

Check out the following video to see the code in action:
```
http://bit.ly/2rbGXqy
```

Setting up your Docker development environment

It's time to get our hands dirty. Let's dive in and set up our workstation. No matter what your preferred OS might be, there's a Docker for that. Using the following as a guide, we will walk you through the setup of Docker on your workstation. We can begin with setting up your Linux workstation, then we'll tackle a Windows system, and finish up with what is probably the most common developer option, the OS X workstation. While OS X may be the most popular developer option, I would recommend that you consider a Linux distribution for your workstation of choice. We'll talk more about why I make that recommendation later in the *Installing Docker on an OS X workstation* section. But for now, just pay close attention during the Linux install discussion in case you are persuaded to develop on Linux.

Generally speaking, there are two flavors of Docker to consider: Docker Enterprise Edition, or Docker EE, and Docker Community Edition, or Docker CE. Typically, in an enterprise, you would opt for the Enterprise Edition, especially for the production environments. It is intended for business-critical use cases, and Docker EE, as the name suggests, is certified, secured, and supported at an enterprise-grade level. It is a commercial solution that is supported by and purchased from Docker.

The other flavor, Docker CE, is a community-supported product. CE is available free and is often the choice for production environments of small businesses, and for developer workstations. Docker CE is a fully capable solution that allows the developer to create containers that can be shared with team members, used with automated build tools for CI/CD, and, if desired, shared with the Docker community at large. As such, it is the ideal option for a developer's workstation. It is worth noting that Docker CE has two release paths: stable and edge. We will be using the stable release path of Docker CE for all of the installation examples in this chapter.

We are going to start off the installation discussion with CentOS Linux, but feel free to skip ahead to the Ubuntu, Windows, or Mac section if you are in a hurry.

Installing Docker on a Linux workstation

We will be executing the Linux installation steps of Docker for both an RPM-based workstation (using CentOS) and a DEB-based workstation (using Ubuntu) so that you will have instructions that fit the Linux distribution that most closely matches what you are currently using, or plan on using at some point in the future. We will begin our installation journey with CentOS.

 You can find all of the download links used in the installation of all OSes in the *References* section.

Installing Docker on a CentOS workstation

Docker CE for CentOS requires a maintained version of CentOS 7. Although installation may work on archived versions, they are neither tested nor supported.

There are three methods to install Docker CE on CentOS:

- Via Docker repositories
- Downloading and manually installing the RPMs
- Running Docker's convenience scripts

The most common method used is via Docker repositories, so let's begin there.

Installing Docker CE via the Docker Repository

First, we will need to install some required packages. Open a terminal window and enter the following command:

```
# installing required packages
sudo yum install -y yum-utils \
  device-mapper-persistent-data \
  lvm2
```

This will make sure that we have both the `yum-config-manager` utility and the device mapper storage driver installed on the system. It is illustrated in the following screenshot:

 Note that your installation of CentOS 7 may already have these installed, and in that case the `yum install` command will report that there is nothing to do.

```
[earl@centos01 ~]$ sudo yum install -y yum-utils \
>    device-mapper-persistent-data \
>    lvm2
[sudo] password for earl:
Loaded plugins: fastestmirror, langpacks
Loading mirror speeds from cached hostfile
 * base: mirror.us.oneandone.net
 * extras: mirror.us.oneandone.net
 * updates: mirror.us.oneandone.net
Package yum-utils-1.1.31-45.el7.noarch already installed and latest version
Package device-mapper-persistent-data-0.7.3-3.el7.x86_64 already installed and latest version
Package 7:lvm2-2.02.177-4.el7.x86_64 already installed and latest version
Nothing to do
[earl@centos01 ~]$ █
```

Next, we will set up the CentOS stable repository for Docker CE.

It is worth noting that you will still need to set up the stable repository even if you want to install the edge releases.

Enter the following command to set up the stable repository:

```
# adding the docker-ce repo
sudo yum-config-manager \
  --add-repo \
  https://download.docker.com/linux/centos/docker-ce.repo
```

Optionally, if you want to use the edge release, you can enable it with the following command:

```
# enable edge releases
sudo yum-config-manager --enable docker-ce-edge
```

Similarly, you can disable access to the edge release with this command:

```
# disable edge releases
sudo yum-config-manager --disable docker-ce-edge
```

Now the fun begins... We are going to install Docker CE. To do so, enter the following command:

```
# install docker
sudo yum -y install docker-ce
```

If you get an error about the need to have container-selinux installed, use this command to install it, then try again:

```
# install container-selinux
sudo yum -y --enablerepo=rhui-REGION-rhel-server-extras \
    install container-selinux

sudo yum -y install docker-ce
```

There you have it! Installing Docker CE was way easier than you thought it was going to be, right?

Let's use the most basic method to confirm a successful install, by issuing the version command.

This command validates that we installed Docker CE, and shows us what version of Docker was just installed. Enter the following command:

```
# validate install with version command
docker --version
```

The latest version of Docker CE, at the time of writing, is 18.03.1:

```
[earl@centos01 ~]$ docker --version
Docker version 18.03.1-ce, build 9ee9f40
[earl@centos01 ~]$
```

We have one more critical step. Although Docker CE is installed, the Docker daemon has not yet been started. To start it, we need to issue the following command:

```
# start docker deamon
sudo systemctl start docker
```

It should quietly start up, looking something like this:

```
[earl@centos01 ~]$ sudo systemctl start docker
[sudo] password for earl:
[earl@centos01 ~]$
```

We saw how to validate that Docker installed using the version command. That is a great quick test, but there is an easy way to confirm not just the install, but that everything started and is working as expected, which is by running our first Docker container.

Let's issue the following command to run the hello-world container:

```
# run a test container
sudo docker run hello-world
```

If all is well, you will see something like the following:

```
[earl@centos01 ~]$ sudo docker run hello-world
[sudo] password for earl:
Unable to find image 'hello-world:latest' locally
latest: Pulling from library/hello-world
9bb5a5d4561a: Pull complete
Digest: sha256:f5233545e43561214ca4891fd1157e1c3c563316ed8e237750d59bde73361e77
Status: Downloaded newer image for hello-world:latest

Hello from Docker!
This message shows that your installation appears to be working correctly.

To generate this message, Docker took the following steps:
 1. The Docker client contacted the Docker daemon.
 2. The Docker daemon pulled the "hello-world" image from the Docker Hub.
    (amd64)
 3. The Docker daemon created a new container from that image which runs the
    executable that produces the output you are currently reading.
 4. The Docker daemon streamed that output to the Docker client, which sent it
    to your terminal.

To try something more ambitious, you can run an Ubuntu container with:
 $ docker run -it ubuntu bash

Share images, automate workflows, and more with a free Docker ID:
 https://hub.docker.com/

For more examples and ideas, visit:
 https://docs.docker.com/engine/userguide/

[earl@centos01 ~]$ █
```

We've got Docker CE installed on our CentOS workstation, and it is already working and running containers. We are off to a great start. Now that we know how to do an install using the Docker repositories, let's have a look at how to manually install using a downloaded RPM.

Installing Docker CE manually using a downloaded RPM

Another way to install Docker CE is to use a downloaded RPM. This method involves downloading the Docker CE RPM for the version you wish to install. You need to browse to the Docker CE Stable RPM downloads site. The URL for this is `https://download.docker.com/linux/centos/7/x86_64/stable/Packages`:

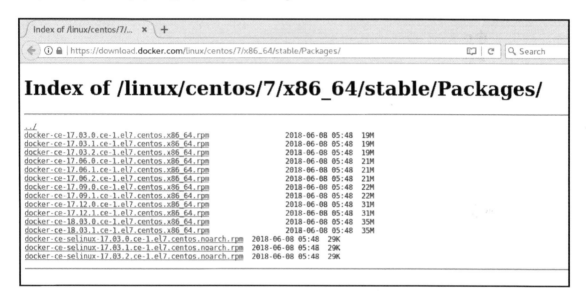

Click on the version of Docker CE you want to download, and when prompted, tell your browser to save the file. Next, issue the `yum install` command, providing the path and filename for the downloaded RPM file. Your command should look something like this:

```
# install the docker rpm
sudo yum install ~/Downloads/docker-ce-18.03.1.ce-1.el7.centos.x86_64.rpm
```

You will need to start the Docker daemon. You'll use the preceding command in the repo section:

```
# start docker
sudo systemctl start docker
```

And, as we learned before, you can validate the functionality of your installation with the following commands:

```
# validate the install and functionality
docker --version
sudo docker run hello-world
```

While this method might seem simpler and easier to execute, it is less desirable because it is more of a manual process, especially when it comes time to update your version of Docker CE. You have to again browse to the downloads page, find the later version, download it, then do the yum install. Using the Docker Repository method described earlier, upgrades are as simple as issuing a yum upgrade command. Let's now take a look at one more method of installing Docker CE on your CentOS workstation.

Installing Docker CE by running convenience scripts

The third way to install Docker is to use the convenience scripts provided by Docker. The scripts allow you to install either the latest edge version or the latest test version of Docker. It is not recommended that either of these is used in a production environment, but they do serve a purpose for testing and developing the latest Docker versions. The scripts are somewhat limited in that they do not allow you to customize any options during the install. The same scripts can be used across a variety of Linux distributions as they determine the base distro you are running and then do the install based on that determination. The process is simple.

Use curl to pull down the desired script, and then use sudo to run the script.

The commands to run the latest edge version are as follows:

```
# download and run the install script
curl -fsSL get.docker.com -o get-docker.sh
sudo sh get-docker.sh
```

Executing the script will result in output that looks like the following:

```
[earl@centos01 ~]$ curl -fsSL get.docker.com -o get-docker.sh
[earl@centos01 ~]$ sudo sh get-docker.sh

We trust you have received the usual lecture from the local System
Administrator. It usually boils down to these three things:

    #1) Respect the privacy of others.
    #2) Think before you type.
    #3) With great power comes great responsibility.

[sudo] password for earl:
# Executing docker install script, commit: 36b78b2
+ sh -c 'yum install -y -q yum-utils'
Package yum-utils-1.1.31-45.el7.noarch already installed and latest version
+ sh -c 'yum-config-manager --add-repo https://download.docker.com/linux/centos/docker-ce.repo'
Loaded plugins: fastestmirror, langpacks
adding repo from: https://download.docker.com/linux/centos/docker-ce.repo
grabbing file https://download.docker.com/linux/centos/docker-ce.repo to /etc/yum.repos.d/docker-ce.repo
repo saved to /etc/yum.repos.d/docker-ce.repo
+ '[' edge '!=' stable ']'
+ sh -c 'yum-config-manager --enable docker-ce-edge'
Loaded plugins: fastestmirror, langpacks
=================================================== repo: docker-ce-edge ===================================================
[docker-ce-edge]
async = True
bandwidth = 0
base_persistdir = /var/lib/yum/repos/x86_64/7
baseurl = https://download.docker.com/linux/centos/7/x86_64/edge
```

The docker group has been created for you by the script, but since CentOS is RPM centric, you still need to start the Docker service yourself:

```
# start docker
sudo systemctl start docker
```

If this were a Debian-based system, the Docker service would have been started automatically by the script.

Now that we have examined the three ways to install Docker on your CentOS workstation, it is a good time to discuss a few additional steps that are recommended in your post-installation setup.

Post-install steps you might want to consider

All three of the install methods automatically create a docker group for you, but if you want to be able to run Docker commands without using root or sudo, then you will want to add your user to the docker group.

Be aware that many Docker commands require full admin access to execute, so adding a user to the docker group is comparable to granting them root access, and the security implications should be considered. If the user already has root access on their workstation, adding them to the docker group is only providing them a convenience.

Adding the current user to the docker group is easily accomplished with the following command:

```
# add the current user to the docker group
sudo usermod -aG docker $USER
```

You will need to log out and log back in to update the group memberships on your account, but once you have done that, you should be all set to execute any Docker commands without using sudo.

This can be validated by running the hello-world container without sudo:

```
# test that sudo is not needed
docker run hello-world
```

Next, you will want to configure your system to have the Docker service start on system-boot:

```
# configure docker to start on boot
sudo systemctl enable docker
```

Another post-install step you should consider is installing docker-compose.

This tool can be an important addition to your Docker tool belt and we will be discussing its use in Chapter 7, *Docker Stacks*. The command to install docker-compose is:

```
# install docker compose
sudo curl -L \
https://github.com/docker/compose/releases/download/1.21.2/docker-compose-$
(uname -s)-$(uname -m) \
  -o /usr/local/bin/docker-compose
sudo chmod +x /usr/local/bin/docker-compose
```

Congratulations, your CentOS workstation is now ready to start developing your Docker images and deploying your Docker containers. Next up, we will learn how to install Docker onto a DEB-based system using an Ubuntu workstation. If you're ready, read on.

Installing Docker on an Ubuntu workstation

As we did on the CentOS workstation, we are going to install Docker CE on our Ubuntu workstation. The requirement for installing Docker CE on Ubuntu is that you have to be running a 64-bit recent LTS release, such as Bionic, Xenial, or Trusty. You can install an edge version of Docker CE onto the Artful version of Ubuntu.

There are three methods to install Docker CE on Ubuntu:

- Via Docker repositories
- Downloading and manually installing the DEB packages
- Running convenience scripts

The most common method used is via Docker repositories, so let's begin there.

Installing Docker CE via the Docker Repository

We need to set up the Docker repository first, and then we can do the installation, so let's take care of the repo now.

The first step will be to update the apt package index. Use the following command to do that:

```
# update apt-get libraries
sudo apt-get update
```

Now we need to install some supporting packages:

```
# install required packages
sudo apt-get install \
   apt-transport-https \
   ca-certificates \
   curl \
   software-properties-common
```

Next, we need to get the GPG key for Docker:

```
# get the GPG key for docker
curl -fsSL https://download.docker.com/linux/ubuntu/gpg | \
   sudo apt-key add -
```

You can confirm that you have added Docker's GPG key successfully; it will have a fingerprint of 9DC8 5822 9FC7 DD38 854A E2D8 8D81 803C 0EBF CD88.

You can verify the key by checking the last eight characters match `0EBFCD88` with this command:

```
# validating the docker GPG key is installed
sudo apt-key fingerprint 0EBFCD88
```

Finally, we need to actually set up the repository. We will be focusing on the stable repo for our examples.

If you want to install the edge or test versions of Docker CE, be sure to add the word `edge` or `test` after the word `stable` (do not replace the word `stable`) in the following command:

```
# adding the docker repository
sudo add-apt-repository \
    "deb [arch=amd64] https://download.docker.com/linux/ubuntu \
    $(lsb_release -cs) \
    stable"
```

Now that our system is set up with the correct repository for installing Docker CE, let's install it.

Start by making sure that all of the packages are up to date by issuing the `apt-get update` command:

```
# update apt-get libraries again
sudo apt-get update
```

And now we will actually install Docker CE:

```
# install docker
sudo apt-get install docker-ce
```

Docker is installed. You can check the Docker version after the install to confirm a successful installation:

```
# validate install with version command
docker --version
```

The version command should look something like this:

```
earl@ubuntu:~$ docker --version
Docker version 18.03.1-ce, build 9ee9f40
earl@ubuntu:~$
```

Now, let's validate that the Docker installation is working as desired. To do this, we will run the hello-world Docker image using the following command:

```
# validating functionality by running a container
sudo docker run hello-world
```

```
earl@ubuntu: ~
earl@ubuntu:~$ sudo docker run hello-world
Unable to find image 'hello-world:latest' locally
latest: Pulling from library/hello-world
9bb5a5d4561a: Pull complete
Digest: sha256:3e1764d0f546ceac4565547df2ac4907fe46f007ea229fd7ef2718514bcec35d
Status: Downloaded newer image for hello-world:latest

Hello from Docker!
This message shows that your installation appears to be working correctly.

To generate this message, Docker took the following steps:
 1. The Docker client contacted the Docker daemon.
 2. The Docker daemon pulled the "hello-world" image from the Docker Hub.
    (amd64)
 3. The Docker daemon created a new container from that image which runs the
    executable that produces the output you are currently reading.
 4. The Docker daemon streamed that output to the Docker client, which sent it
    to your terminal.

To try something more ambitious, you can run an Ubuntu container with:
 $ docker run -it ubuntu bash

Share images, automate workflows, and more with a free Docker ID:
 https://hub.docker.com/

For more examples and ideas, visit:
 https://docs.docker.com/engine/userguide/

earl@ubuntu:~$
```

Did you notice something interesting happened?

We did not have to start Docker after the installation as we did in the CentOS installation. That is because, on DEB-based Linux systems, the install process also starts Docker for us. Additionally, the Ubuntu workstation is configured to start Docker on boot. So both of the Docker start steps are handled for you during the installation. Nice! Your Ubuntu workstation now has Docker installed and we've verified it is working as desired.

Although using the Docker repository is the best way to install Docker on your workstation, let's take a quick look at another way to install Docker CE on an Ubuntu workstation, that being by manually installing it with a DEB package.

Installing Docker CE manually using a DEB package

Now we will show you how to download and install the Docker CE DEB package. You should consider using this method if, for whatever reason, the repositories are not available for your workstation.

You will need to download the Docker CE package, so start by opening your browser and going to the Ubuntu Docker CE packages download site at `https://download.docker.com/linux/ubuntu/dists/`.

There, you will find a list of Ubuntu version folders listed, which looks something like this:

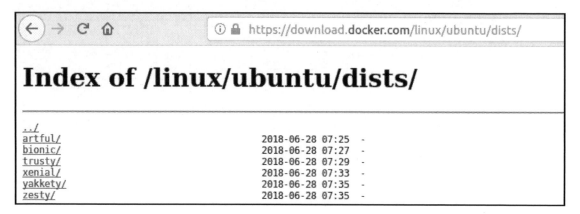

You want to select the folder that matches the version of Ubuntu installed on your workstation, which in my case is the `xenial` folder.

Continue browsing to `/pool/stable/` and then to the processor folder that matches your workstation hardware. For me that is amd64, and it looks like this:

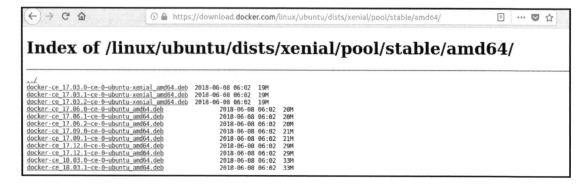

Now click on the version of Docker CE you want to download and install.

Be sure to select the **Save File** option before you click **OK**.

Once the package has been downloaded to your workstation, to install it, just use the dpkg command for manually installing a package.

You provide the path and filename for the downloaded Docker CE package as a parameter to dpkg. Here is the command I used for the package that was just downloaded:

```
# installing docker package
sudo dpkg -i ~/Downloads/docker-ce_18.03.1~ce-0~ubuntu_amd64.deb
```

Executing the command looks like this:

```
earl@ubuntu: ~

earl@ubuntu:~$ ll ~/Downloads
total 33256
drwxr-xr-x  2 earl earl     4096 Jun 29 22:02 ./
drwxr-xr-x 17 earl earl     4096 Jun 29 21:46 ../
-rw-rw-r--  1 earl earl 34045202 Jun 29 22:02 docker-ce_18.03.1~ce-0~ubuntu_amd64.deb
earl@ubuntu:~$ sudo dpkg -i ~/Downloads/docker-ce_18.03.1~ce-0~ubuntu_amd64.deb
Selecting previously unselected package docker-ce.
(Reading database ... 245646 files and directories currently installed.)
Preparing to unpack .../docker-ce_18.03.1~ce-0~ubuntu_amd64.deb ...
Unpacking docker-ce (18.03.1~ce-0~ubuntu) ...
Setting up docker-ce (18.03.1~ce-0~ubuntu) ...
Processing triggers for systemd (229-4ubuntu21.2) ...
Processing triggers for ureadahead (0.100.0-19) ...
Processing triggers for man-db (2.7.5-1) ...
earl@ubuntu:~$
```

Now that Docker is installed, let's use the version command to confirm successful install, and then run the hello-world container to validate that Docker is working as desired:

```
# validating the install and functionality
docker --version
sudo docker run hello-world
```

This is good. Just like the repository installation, your docker group has been created and both of the start steps are handled for you in the manual package installation. You do not have to start Docker, and you do not have to configure Docker to start on boot. So, you are ready to start creating Docker images and running Docker containers.

However, before we get going with creating and running, there is one more method of installing Docker on an Ubuntu workstation that we will cover. You can use Docker's convenience scripts to install the latest edge or test versions of Docker CE. Let's take a look at how to do that now.

Installing Docker CE by running convenience scripts

Another method of installing Docker is to use the convenience scripts provided by Docker. The scripts allow you to install either the latest edge version or the latest test version of Docker. It is not recommended that either of these is used in a production environment, however, they do serve a purpose for testing and developing the latest Docker versions. The scripts are somewhat limited in that they do not allow you to customize any options in the install. The same scripts can be used across a variety of Linux distributions as they determine the base distro you are running, and then do the install based on that determination. The process is simple. Use `curl` to pull down the desired script, and then use sudo to run the script. The commands to run the latest edge version are as follows.

Use the following command to install curl:

```
# install curl
sudo apt-get install curl
```

Now get the script and run the docker script to install:

```
# download and run the docker install script
curl -fsSL get.docker.com -o get-docker.sh
sudo sh get-docker.sh
```

Executing the script will result in output that looks like the following:

```
earl@ubuntu:~$ curl -fsSL get.docker.com -o get-docker.sh
earl@ubuntu:~$ sudo sh get-docker.sh
# Executing docker install script, commit: 36b78b2
+ sh -c apt-get update -qq >/dev/null
+ sh -c apt-get install -y -qq apt-transport-https ca-certificates curl >/dev/null
+ sh -c curl -fsSL "https://download.docker.com/linux/ubuntu/gpg" | apt-key add -qq - >/dev/null
+ sh -c echo "deb [arch=amd64] https://download.docker.com/linux/ubuntu xenial edge" > /etc/apt/sources.list.d/docker.list
+ [ ubuntu = debian ]
+ sh -c apt-get update -qq >/dev/null
+ sh -c apt-get install -y -qq --no-install-recommends docker-ce >/dev/null
+ sh -c docker version
Client:
 Version:      18.05.0-ce
 API version:  1.37
 Go version:   go1.9.5
 Git commit:   f150324
 Built:        Wed May  9 22:16:25 2018
 OS/Arch:      linux/amd64
 Experimental: false
 Orchestrator: swarm

Server:
 Engine:
  Version:      18.05.0-ce
  API version:  1.37 (minimum version 1.12)
  Go version:   go1.9.5
```

The docker group has been created for you by the script. The Docker service has been started, and the workstation has been configured to run Docker on boot. So, once again, you are ready to start using Docker.

We have examined the three ways to install Docker on your Ubuntu workstation, so now is a good time to discuss an additional step that is recommended for your post-installation setup.

Post-install steps you might want to consider

All three of these install methods automatically create a docker group for you, but if you want to be able to run Docker commands without using `root` or sudo, you will want to add your user to the docker group.

 Be aware that many Docker commands require full admin access to execute, so adding a user to the docker group is comparable to granting them root access, and the security implications should be considered. If the user already has root access on their workstation, adding them to the docker group is only providing them a convenience.

Adding the current user to the docker group is easily accomplished with the following command:

```
# add the current user to the docker group
sudo usermod -aG docker $USER
```

You will need to log out and log back in to update the group memberships on your account, but once you have done that, you should be all set to execute any Docker commands without using sudo.

This can be validated with the hello-world container:

```
# validate that sudo is no longer needed
docker run hello-world
```

Another post-install step you should consider is installing docker-compose.

This tool can be an important addition to your Docker tool belt and we will be discussing its use in Chapter 7, *Docker Stacks*. The command to install docker-compose is:

```
# install docker-compose
sudo curl -L
https://github.com/docker/compose/releases/download/1.21.2/docker-compose-$
(uname -s)-$(uname -m) -o /usr/local/bin/docker-compose
sudo chmod +x /usr/local/bin/docker-compose
```

Congratulations, your Ubuntu workstation is now ready to start developing your Docker images and deploying your Docker containers. Next up, we will learn how to install Docker onto a Windows-based workstation. If you're ready, read on.

Installing Docker on a Windows workstation

The Windows version of Docker CE is compatible with Windows 10 Pro or Enterprise editions. Docker CE on Windows provides a complete Docker development solution by integrating with Windows Hyper-V virtualization and networking. Docker CE on Windows supports creating and running both Windows and Linux containers. Docker CE on Windows is available from the Docker store at `https://store.docker.com/editions/community/docker-ce-desktop-windows`.

You will need to log in to the Docker store to download the Docker CE for Windows installer, so if you don't already have an account, go ahead and create one now and then log in to it.

 Be sure to save your Docker credentials securely as you will be using them a lot in the future.

After logging in, you should see the **Get Docker** download button. Click on the download button and allow the installer to download to your workstation. Once the installer has finished downloading, you can click the **Run** button to begin the installation. If you get the security check, confirm that you want to run the installer executable by clicking the **Run** button. If you have UAC enabled on your workstation, you may see the User Account Control warning asking you to confirm that you want to allow the Docker CE installer to make changes to your device. You have to check **Yes** to continue, so go ahead and click it now.

The Docker CE installer will run and it will begin downloading Docker. Once the Docker installation files have been successfully downloaded, the installer will ask you to confirm your desired configuration. The options here are few. It is my recommendation that you add the shortcut to the desktop and that you do not check the Use Windows containers instead of Linux containers option:

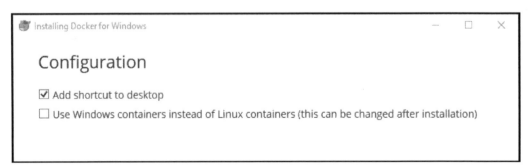

The installer will unpack the Docker CE files. When the files are unpacked, you will get the Installation succeeded notification. According to the current documentation, the installer will run Docker for you at the end of the installation. It has been my experience that it does not always happen. Be patient and give it time, but if it does not start that first time you may have to run Docker manually.

If you selected the configuration option to add a shortcut for Docker to your desktop, you will now be able to double-click that shortcut icon and start Docker for the first time.

Docker will run and you will get a Welcome screen that lets you know that Docker is up and running. It is recommended that you provide your Docker credentials and log in at this time.

Whenever Docker is running, you will see a whale icon in the taskbar notifications area. If you mouse over that icon, you can get the status of the Docker process. You will see such statuses as **Docker is starting** and **Docker is running**. You can right-click on the icon to bring up the Docker for Windows menu:

Once you have Docker running on your Windows workstation, you can open up a Windows PowerShell command window and start using Docker. To verify that the installation was completed successfully, open a PowerShell window and enter the version command. To confirm that Docker is working as desired, run the hello-world Docker container:

```
# validate install and functionality
docker --version
docker run hello-world
```

Your Windows 10 workstation is now set up to create Docker images and run Docker containers. Docker should also be configured to start up on boot so that when you need to reboot your workstation, it will start up automatically.

Be aware that using Docker CE on a Windows workstation is not exactly like using Docker CE on a Linux workstation. There is an additional layer of virtualization this is hidden behind the scenes. Docker is running a small Linux VM in Hyper-V and all of your Docker interactions are passed through, to, and from, this Linux VM. For most use cases, this is never going to present any issues, but it does affect performance. We will talk more about this in the *Discovering the differences to watch out for between OSes* section.

There is one more bit of setup that we want to take a look at, so if you are ready, jump right into the next section.

Post-install steps you might want to consider

Here are a couple of post-install steps I recommend for your Docker Windows workstation.

Installing Kitematic

The Windows installation of Docker CE integrates with a graphical user interface tool called Kitematic. If you are a graphical interface kind of person (and since you are using Windows for Docker, I will guess that you are), you will want to install this tool.

Find the `Docker` icon in the taskbar notifications area and right-click on it to bring up the Docker for Windows menu. Click on the **Kitematic** menu option. Kitematic is not installed by default. You have to download the archive that contains the application. When you click the **Kitematic** menu option for the first time, you will be prompted to download it. Click the **Download** button, and save the archive file to your workstation:

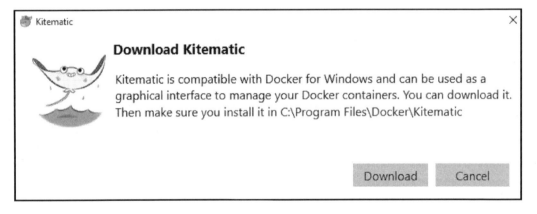

You will need to unzip the Kitematic archive to use it. The uncompressed Kitematic folder needs to be in the `C:\Program Files\Docker` folder with a folder name of `Kitematic` for the Docker submenu integration to work correctly. Once you have Kitematic installed in the correct path on your Windows workstation, you can right-click the `Docker` icon in the task bar notifications area and select the Kitematic option again.

You will be prompted to enter your Docker credentials again to connect to Docker Hub. You can skip this step, but it is my recommendation that you go ahead and log in now. Once you log in (or skip the login step), you will see the Kitematic user interface. It allows you to download and run Docker containers on your workstation. Go ahead and try one, such as the *hello-world-nginx* container, or if you want to play a game, try the Minecraft container.

You are now ready to create Docker images and run Docker containers in your Windows 10 workstation, but we have one more workstation OS to learn how to install Docker CE on. Let's look at installing it on an OS X workstation next.

Setting up DockerCompletion for PowerShell

If you have ever used command-line completion, you will want to consider installing DockerCompletion for PowerShell. This tool provides command-line completion for Docker commands. It is fairly easy to install. You will need your system set up to allow the execution of the downloaded module. To do this, open a PowerShell command window with **Run as Administrator**, and issue the following command:

```
# allow remote signed scripts to run
Set-ExecutionPolicy RemoteSigned
```

You can now close the Administrator command window and open a normal user PowerShell command window. To install the DockerCompletion module, issue this command:

```
# install Docker completion
Install-Module DockerCompletion -Scope CurrentUser
```

And finally, to activate the module in your current PowerShell window, use this command:

```
# enable Docker completion
Import-Module DockerCompletion
```

Now you can use the features of command completion for all your Docker commands. This is a great keystroke saver!

 Note that the Import-Module command is only active in the current PowerShell command window. If you want to have it available to all future PowerShell sessions, you will need to add the Import-Module DockerCompletion to your PowerShell profile.

You can easily edit your PowerShell profile (or create a new one if you haven't already) with this command:

```
# update your user profile to enable docker completion for every PowerShell
command prompt
notepad $PROFILE
```

Enter the `Import-Module DockerCompletion` command and save the profile. Now your Docker command-line completion feature will be active in all future PowerShell sessions.

Installing Docker on an OS X workstation

The story for Docker on Mac has advanced a lot in recent years, and it is now a real, usable development solution for your Mac workstation. Docker CE for Mac requires OS X El Capitan 10.11 or newer macOS releases. The Docker CE app integrates with the hypervisor, network, and filesystem built into OS X. The installation process is simple: download the Docker installer image and launch it. You can download the installer image from the Docker store. You must log in to the Docker store be able to download the install image, so, create an account there if you don't have one already.

 Be sure to save your credentials securely as you will need them later.

Browse to the Docker store page for Docker CE for Mac at `https://store.docker.com/editions/community/docker-ce-desktop-mac`. Remember that you must log into the Docker store to be able to download the installer image.

Once logged in to the Docker store, the **Get Docker** button will be available to click. Go ahead and click on it to start the download. The Docker CE for Mac install image may take some time to download. When the download has completed, double-click on the `Docker.dmg` image file to mount and open it:

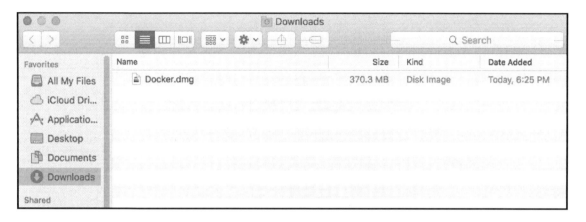

Once the Docker CE for Mac image has mounted and opened, click the `Docker` icon and drag it onto the `Applications` icon to complete the install. The copying `Docker` to `Applications` action will be initiated. And when the copy process completes, the Docker application will be available to run from your `Applications` folder. Double-click on your `Docker` icon to launch it. Launching Docker for the first time will caution you that you are running an application downloaded from the internet to make sure you really want to open it. When the Docker app opens, you will be greeted with a friendly **Welcome to Docker** message.

Clicking next on the welcome message will warn you that Docker requires elevated privileges to run and will inform you that you must provide your credentials to install Docker's networking and app links. Enter your username and password. The Docker application will launch, adding a whale icon to the menu-notification area.

You will also be prompted to enter Docker store credentials to allow Docker for Mac to log in to the store. Enter your credentials and click on the `Log In` button. You will get a confirmation showing that you are currently logged in.

To validate that our installation was successful and confirm the functionality of our installation, we will issue the version command and then run Docker's hello-world container:

```
# validate install and functionality
docker --version
docker run hello-world
```

Your macOS workstation is now set up to create Docker images and run Docker containers. You are ready to containerize your apps! You can easily use your terminal window for all of your Docker work, but you may be interested in the graphical UI tool that is available for Mac, called **Kitematic**. Let's install Kitematic next.

Post-install steps you might want to consider

Here are a couple of post-install steps I recommend for your Docker OS X workstation.

Installing Kitematic

Although you can use the Docker CLI in your OS X terminal window, and probably will do so for most of your Docker development work, you have the option of using a graphical UI tool called Kitematic instead. To install Kitematic, right-click on the whale icon in the OS X menu-notification area to open the Docker for Mac menu. Click on the **Kitematic** menu option to download (and later to run) the Kitematic application. If you have not yet installed Kitematic, when you click on the Docker for Mac menu for it, you will be shown a message that includes a download link. The message also reminds you that you must install Kitematic into your `Applications` folder to enable Docker menu-integration. Click the **here** link to download the Kitematic application:

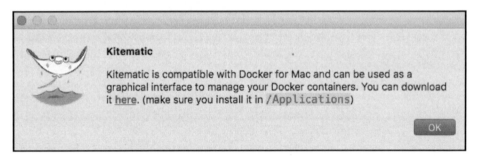

Once the download completes, move the downloaded application into your `Applications` folder, as directed earlier. Then, using the Docker for Mac menu, click on the **Kitematic** menu option again. This time it will run the Kitematic application. The first time you run the application, you will get the standard warning that you are running something that has been downloaded from the internet, asking if you really want to open it. Click on the **Open** button to do so.

Once you have Kitematic installed on your Mac workstation, you can click the Docker whale icon in the menu bar notifications area and select the Kitematic option again.

You will be prompted to enter your Docker credentials to connect Kitematic to Docker Hub. You can skip this step, but it is my recommendation that you go ahead and log in now. Once you log in (or skip the login step), you will see the Kitematic user interface. This allows you to download and run Docker containers on your workstation. Go ahead and try one, such as the *hello-world-nginx* container, or if you want to play a game, try the Minecraft container.

Congratulations! You are now set up to use both the Docker CLI and the Kitematic graphical UI to run your Docker containers and manage your Docker images. However, you will do your Docker image creation using the OS X terminal and your favorite code editor.

Installing Docker command-line completion

Install Homebrew. You may (probably) already have Homebrew installed on your Mac, but if not, you should install it now. Here is the command to install it:

```
# install homebrew
/usr/bin/ruby -e "$(curl -fsSL
https://raw.githubusercontent.com/Homebrew/install/master/install)"
```

Next, use Homebrew to install `bash-completion`. Here is the command:

```
# use homebrew to install bash completion
brew install bash-completion
```

The installation of `bash-completion` will instruct you to add the following line to your `~/.bash_profile` file:

```
# update the bash profile to enable bash completion for every terminal
session
[ -f /usr/local/etc/bash_completion ] && . /usr/local/etc/bash_completion
```

Now, create the links necessary to enable the Docker command-line completion feature. There is one link for each of the Docker toolsets. Here are the link commands for bash (if you use `zsh`, check the next code block for the link commands):

```
# create links for bash shell
ln -s /Applications/Docker.app/Contents/Resources/etc/docker.bash-
completion $(brew --prefix)/etc/bash_completion.d/docker
ln -s /Applications/Docker.app/Contents/Resources/etc/docker-machine.bash-
completion $(brew --prefix)/etc/bash_completion.d/docker-machine
ln -s /Applications/Docker.app/Contents/Resources/etc/docker-compose.bash-
completion $(brew --prefix)/etc/bash_completion.d/docker-compose
```

Note that if you are using `zsh` instead of bash, the link commands are different. Here are the link commands for `zsh`:

```
# create links for zsh shell
ln -s /Applications/Docker.app/Contents/Resources/etc/docker.zsh-completion
/usr/local/share/zsh/site-functions/_docker
ln -s /Applications/Docker.app/Contents/Resources/etc/docker-machine.zsh-
completion /usr/local/share/zsh/site-functions/_docker-machine
```

```
ln -s /Applications/Docker.app/Contents/Resources/etc/docker-compose.zsh-
completion /usr/local/share/zsh/site-functions/_docker-compose
```

Finally, restart your terminal session—you can now use Docker command completion! Try it by typing `docker` and hitting the *Tab* key twice.

References

- Docker Enterprise Edition data: `https://www.docker.com/enterprise-edition`
- Docker Community Edition data: `https://www.docker.com/community-edition`
- Download Docker CE for CentOS: `https://store.docker.com/editions/community/docker-ce-server-centos`
- Download Docker CE for Ubuntu: `https://store.docker.com/editions/community/docker-ce-server-ubuntu`
- Download Docker CE for Windows: `https://store.docker.com/editions/community/docker-ce-desktop-windows`
- Download Docker CE for Mac: `https://store.docker.com/editions/community/docker-ce-desktop-mac`
- The Docker CE Stable RPM download site for CentOS: `https://download.docker.com/linux/centos/7/x86_64/stable/Packages`
- The Docker Install Repo: `https://github.com/docker/docker-install`
- The Docker CE DEB package download site for Ubuntu: `https://download.docker.com/linux/ubuntu/dists/`
- Running Windows Docker containers on Windows: `https://blog.docker.com/2016/09/build-your-first-docker-windows-server-container/`
- DockerCompletion for PowerShell: `https://github.com/matt9ucci/DockerCompletion`
- Docker CE for Mac: `https://store.docker.com/editions/community/docker-ce-desktop-mac`
- Command-line completion for Mac: `https://docs.docker.com/docker-for-mac/#install-shell-completion`
- Installing Homebrew on your Mac: `https://brew.sh/`

What differences to watch out for between OSes

Docker images, by design, are self-contained packages that include everything needed to run the application they are designed to execute. One of the great strengths of Docker is that Docker images can be run on almost any operating system. That being said, there are some differences in the experience of running Docker images on different OSes. Docker was created on Linux and is deeply integrated with some key Linux constructs. So, as you would expect, when you run Docker on Linux, everything integrates directly and seamlessly with the OS. Docker leverages the Linux kernel and filesystem natively.

Unfortunately, when you run Docker for Windows or Docker for Mac, Docker cannot leverage the same constructs that it does natively on Linux because they just do not exist on these other OSes. Docker handles this by creating a small, efficient Linux VM in a hypervisor for the non-Linux OS. With Docker for Windows, this Linux VM is created in Hyper-V. On macOS, the VM is created in a custom hypervisor, called **hyperkit**.

As you might expect, there is a performance overhead associated with the helper VMs. However, if you do use Windows or OS X for your development workstation, you will be pleased to know that Docker has made a lot of positive strides on both platforms, reducing the overhead and improving performance significantly with each new major version released. There are a lot of reports of high CPU utilization for the hyperkit hypervisor on OS X, but I have not personally experienced the issue. With the current stable versions of Docker CE, I believe that both Windows and OS X can be successfully used for Docker development.

Still, there are other differences, besides processing performance, to consider. There are two that you should be aware of: file mounts and endpoints.

Docker CE on a Linux OS is able to directly use the filesystem for its file mounts in the running containers—this provides native-disk-performance levels. You also can change the filesystem drivers used to achieve different levels of performance. This is not available for Docker on Windows or Docker on Mac. For both Windows and OS X, there is an additional filesystem tool that handles the file mounts. On Windows, you will be using Windows shared files, and on OS X it is **osxfs**. Unfortunately for the Windows and OS X users, the performance hit on the file mounts is significant. Even though Docker has made leaps and bounds in improving the file mount story for Windows and for OS X with version 17 and later, both are still measurably slower compared to running natively on a Linux OS. For Windows specifically, the file mount options are very restrictive. If you are developing an application that is disk-utilization heavy, this difference might be enough to have you immediately consider switching to a Linux development workstation.

One other area that differs between Docker on Linux and Docker for Windows or Docker for Mac is the utilization of endpoint ports. One example is with Docker for Windows; you are not able to access a container's endpoint from its the host using localhost. This is a known bug, but the only workaround is to access your container's endpoints from a different host than you are running them on. With Docker for Mac, there are other endpoint limitations, such as not being able to ping a container (because Docker for Mac cannot route the ping traffic to and from the container) and you cannot have per-container IP addressing (because the Docker bridge network is not reachable from macOS).

Any of these limitations might be enough for you to consider switching your development workstation to an Ubuntu or CentOS operating system. It was for me, and you will find that most of the examples found in this book will be executed on my Ubuntu workstation. I will try to point out any areas that may be significantly different if you are using Windows or OS X.

Summary

Wow! We covered a lot in this first chapter. You should now be able to install Docker on your workstation, regardless of the OS that it is running. You should be able to install Docker onto a Linux workstation using three different methods, and know some of the differences between installing on an RPM-based system and a DEB-based system.

We also covered some very significant reasons why you might consider using a Linux workstation for your development, instead of using a Windows or macOS workstation. And by now, you should be able to easily validate the successful installation of Docker by checking the version of Docker installed.

You should be able to easily confirm that Docker is working as desired by running a hello-world container. Not bad for your first chapter, right? Well, with this foundation, and your newly Docker-ready workstation, let's move right into Chapter 2, *Learning Docker Commands*, where we will learn about many Docker commands you'll use every day.

References

- Docker for Windows limitations: https://docs.docker.com/docker-for-windows/troubleshoot/#limitations-of-windows-containers-for-localhost-and-published-ports
- Docker for Mac limitations: https://docs.docker.com/v17.09/docker-for-mac/networking/#known-limitations-use-cases-and-workarounds

2
Learning Docker Commands

In this chapter, we will learn some essential Docker commands. While we focus on one of the most important commands, the `container run` command, we will also cover many other commands that you will be using every day. These commands include the list container command, the stop container command, and the remove container command. Along the way, we will also discover other container commands such as logs, inspect, stats, attach, exec, and commit. I think you will find this chapter to be an excellent foundation for Docker education.

> *BIC: The Bureau of International des Containers was founded in 1933 as a neutral, non-profit, international organization whose mission is to promote the safe, secure, and sustainable expansion of containerization and intermodal transportation.*

By the end of this chapter, you will know the following:

- The current and previous command-line syntax
- Both ways to use the version commands
- How to use the `container run` command and many of its optional parameters
- How to start and stop your containers, view information about your containers, interact with running containers, and how to save and reuse changes made to your containers

Technical requirements

You will be pulling Docker images from Docker's public repo, and installing the jq software package, so basic internet access is required to execute the examples within this chapter.

The code files of this chapter can be found on GitHub:
https://github.com/PacktPublishing/Docker-Quick-Start-Guide/tree/master/Chapter02

Check out the following video to see the code in action:
`http://bit.ly/2P43WNT`

Information about command syntax

Before we dive into learning about Docker commands and their many options, I want to inform you of a change to the Docker CLI that happened in January 2017.

The number of commands and associated options have been increasing with each new release of Docker. Docker decided that the complexity this was creating needed to be addressed. So, with the release of Docker version 1.13 (Docker also changed the version numbing scheme in 2017), the CLI commands have been divided into management functional groups. For example, there is now a container management group of commands, and an image management group of commands. This changes how you run Docker commands. Here is an example of the use of the old and new `run` command:

```
# the new command syntax...
docker container run hello-world
# the old command syntax...
docker run hello-world
```

This change provides better command organization, but also adds some verbosity to the command line. It's a trade-off. For now, as far as I know, the old command syntax still works for all Docker commands, but for the rest of the examples in this book, I am planning to use the new syntax. At least I'll try, as old habits die hard.

One other note I would like to make here is that most command options have a short and long format. I will try to share the long format as an option in my examples at least once so you will know what the short version stands for. If you installed the Docker command-line completion, it will be a helpful resource for remembering both the new Docker management-based commands and the parameters that can be used with them. Here is a look at the top-level command-completion help for the container commands:

```
→ repos docker container █
attach    -- Attach to a running container
commit    -- Create a new image from a container's changes
cp        -- Copy files/folders between a container and the local filesystem
create    -- Create a new container
diff      -- Inspect changes on a container's filesystem
exec      -- Run a command in a running container
export    -- Export a container's filesystem as a tar archive
inspect   -- Display detailed information on one or more containers
kill      -- Kill one or more running containers
logs      -- Fetch the logs of a container
ls        -- List containers
pause     -- Pause all processes within one or more containers
port      -- List port mappings or a specific mapping for the container
prune     -- Remove all stopped containers
rename    -- Rename a container
restart   -- Restart one or more containers
rm        -- Remove one or more containers
run       -- Run a command in a new container
start     -- Start one or more stopped containers
stats     -- Display a live stream of container(s) resource usage statistics
stop      -- Stop one or more running containers
```

That command list gives us a sneak peek at some of the commands we are going to review in this chapter, so let's get started with learning Docker commands. In Chapter 1, *Setting up a Docker Development Environment*, we used two very common Docker commands: the version command and the run command. While you think you know pretty much everything there is to know about the version command, you may be surprised to learn that it has another trick up its sleeve. There is another version of Docker's version command.

The version command

You have already used the docker --version command as a quick test to confirm that Docker was installed. Now try the command without the dashes:

```
docker version
```

This version of the command gives you greater detail about the version of Docker installed on your system. It is worth noting that the docker-compose command, which we will talk about later, also has two versions of the version command—one with the dashes providing a single-line response, and one without the dashes that delivers more details.

Remember that all the Docker commands have a rich help system built in. Try it by entering any part of a Docker command and using the `--help` parameter. For example, `docker container run --help`.

The Docker run command

Since we will be using the `run` command a lot, we should take a look at that now. You have already used the `run` command in its most basic form:

```
# new syntax
# Usage: docker container run [OPTIONS] IMAGE [COMMAND] [ARG...]
docker container run hello-world

# old syntax
docker run hello-world
```

This command tells Docker that you want to run a container based on the image described as hello-world. You may be asking yourself, did the hello-world container image get installed when I installed Docker? The answer is no. The `docker run` command will look at the local container image cache to see whether there is a container image that matches the description of the requested container. If there is, Docker will run the container from the cached image. If the desired container image is not found in the cache, Docker will reach out to a Docker registry to try to download the container image, storing it in the local cache in the process. Docker will then run the newly-downloaded container from the cache.

A Docker registry is just a centralized location to store and retrieve Docker images. We will talk more about registries and the Docker registry specifically later. For now, just understand that there is a local image cache and a remote image store. You saw the container not found locally process occur when we ran the hello-world container in Chapter 1, *Setting up a Docker Development Environment.* Here is what it looks like when Docker does not find the container image in the local cache and has to download it from the registry:

```
➜  repos docker run hello-world
Unable to find image 'hello-world:latest' locally
latest: Pulling from library/hello-world
9db2ca6ccae0: Pull complete
Digest: sha256:4b8ff392a12ed9ea17784bd3c9a8b1fa3299cac44aca35a85c90c5e3c7afacdc
Status: Downloaded newer image for hello-world:latest
```

You can pre-seed the local docker cache with container images you plan to run by using the docker `pull` command; for example:

```
# new syntax
# Usage: docker image pull [OPTIONS] NAME[:TAG|@DIGEST]
docker image pull hello-world

# old syntax
docker pull hello-world
```

If you prefetch the container image with a `pull` command, when you execute the docker `run` command, it will find the image in the local cache and not need to download it again.

You may have noticed in the preceding screenshot that you requested the hello-world container image and Docker unsuccessfully searched the local cache and then downloaded the `hello-world:latest` container image from the repository. Each container image description is made up of three parts:

- Docker registry host name
- Slash-separated name
- Tag name

The first part, the registry host name, we have not seen or used yet, but it was included via a default value of the public Docker registry. Whenever you do not specify a registry host name, Docker will invisibly use the public Docker registry. This registry host name is `docker.io`. The contents of the Docker registry can be browsed at `https://hub.docker.com/explore`. This is the main public store for Docker images. It is possible to set up and use other public or private image registries, and many corporations will do just that, setting up their own private Docker image registry. We will talk a little more about that in Chapter 8, *Docker and Jenkins*. For now, just understand that the first part of a Docker image description is the registry host name that hosts the container image. It is worth noting that the registry host name can include a port number. This can be used for registries that are configured to serve data on a non-default port value.

The second part of the container image description is the slash-separated name. This part is like a path to, and name of, the container image. There are certain official container images that do not need to specify the path. For those images, you can simply specify the name portion of the slash-separated name. In our example, that is the hello-world part of the description.

The third part of the container image description is the tag name. This part is considered the version tag for the image, but it does not need to be made up of just numbers. The tag name can be any set of ASCII characters, including uppercase and lowercase letters, numbers, dashes, underscores, or periods. About the only restrictions on tag names are that they cannot start with a period or dash, and have to be 128 characters or fewer. The tag name is separated from the slash-separated name by a colon. This brings us back to the `hello-world:latest` image description we saw earlier. Like the registry host name, there is a default value for the tag name. That default value is `latest`. In our example, the tag name being used is the default, and it is shown in the search and download as `hello-world:latest`. You can see all of this in action in the following example:

We confirmed that our local image cache is empty, with the `docker images` command, and we then pulled the fully qualified hello-world image to prefetch it into our local cache. Then we used the same short description as we did in all of our previous hello-world examples, and Docker runs the container without downloading again, showing that the default values are used and that they match the fully-qualified values.

Okay, now that we have all of the basics of the Docker `run` command out of the way, let's dig a little deeper and examine some of the optional parameters that you can use with the `run` command. If you look at the full `run` command syntax, you will see this:

```
# Usage: docker container run [OPTIONS] IMAGE [COMMAND] [ARG...]
```

Note that the last parts of the command are [COMMAND] [ARG...]. This tells us that the container run command has an optional command parameter that can also include its own optional parameters. Docker container images are built with a default command that is executed when you run a container based on the image. For the hello-world container, the default command is /hello. For a full Ubuntu OS container, the default command is bash. Whenever you run an Ubuntu container and don't specify a command to run in the container, the default command will be used. Don't worry if this doesn't make much sense yet—we will cover the default command and overriding it at runtime later in this chapter in the *Back to the Docker run command* section. For now, it is enough to know that when you run a container, it will execute a command that is either the default command or, if provided to the container run command, an override command to execute in the running container. One last note: when the command being executed by the running container (either default or override) terminates, the container will exit. In our examples using the hello-world container, as soon as the /hello command terminates inside the container, the hello-world container exits. In a moment, you will learn more about the difference between a running container and one that has exited.

For now, we will continue our run command discussion with one of my favorite optional parameters, the --rm parameter. A little background information is required here. As you may recall from Chapter 1, *Setting up a Docker Development Environment*, a Docker image is made up of layers. Whenever you run a docker container, it is really just using the locally-cached docker image (which is a stack of layers), and creating a new layer on top that is a read/write layer. All of the execution and changes that occur during the running of a container are stored in its own read/write layer.

The list container command

The indication of a running container can be shown using the following command:

```
# Usage: docker container ls [OPTIONS]
docker container ls
```

This is the list containers command, and without any additional parameters, it will list the currently-running containers. What do I mean by currently running? A container is a special process running on the system, and like other processes on the system, a container can stop or exit. However, unlike other types of processes on your system, the default behavior for a container is to leave behind its read/write layer when it stops. This is because you can restart the container if desired, keeping the state data it had when it exited. As an example, imagine you run a container that is an OS, such as Ubuntu, and in that container you install `wget`. After the container exits, you can restart it, and it will still have `wget` installed. Remember that each running container has its own read/write layer, so, if you run one Ubuntu container and install `wget`, then you run another Ubuntu container, it will not have `wget`. The read/write layers are not shared between containers. However, if you restart a container that had the `wget` installed, it will still be installed.

So, the difference between a running container and a stopped one is that the process is either running or it has exited, leaving behind its own read/write layer. There is a parameter to the list containers command that allows you to list all of the containers, both those running and those that have exited. As you may have guessed, it is the `--all` parameter, and it looks like this:

```
# short form of the parameter is -a
docker container ls -a
# long form is --all
docker container ls --all

# old syntax
docker ps -a
```

Now, let's go back to one of my favorite optional run command parameters, the `--rm` parameter:

```
# there is no short form of the --rm parameter
docker container run --rm hello-world
```

This parameter instructs Docker to remove the container's read/write layer automatically when the container exits. When you run a docker container without the `--rm` parameter, the container data is left behind when the container exits so that the container can be restarted again later. If, however, you include the `--rm` parameter when you run a container, all of the container's read/write data is removed at the time the container exits. This parameter provides an easy clean up on `exit` function that you will often find very helpful. Let's see this with a quick example using the run and `container ls` commands we just discussed:

```
→ repos docker images
REPOSITORY          TAG             IMAGE ID        CREATED         SIZE
hello-world         latest          2cb0d9787c4d    3 days ago      1.85kB
→ repos docker container ls -a
CONTAINER ID        IMAGE           COMMAND         CREATED         STATUS          PORTS           NAMES
→ repos docker container run --rm hello-world > /dev/null
→ repos docker container ls -a
CONTAINER ID        IMAGE           COMMAND         CREATED         STATUS          PORTS           NAMES
→ repos docker container run hello-world > /dev/null
→ repos docker container ls -a
CONTAINER ID        IMAGE           COMMAND         CREATED         STATUS                  PORTS       NAMES
cd828234194a        hello-world     "/hello"        4 seconds ago   Exited (0) 2 seconds ago            competent_payne
→ repos ▐
```

First, we confirmed we had the hello-world image in our local cache. Next, we listed all of the containers on our system, both running and exited. Note the distinction between images and containers. If you are familiar with VMware, the analogy would be somewhat like a template and a VM. Next, we ran the hello-world container using the `--rm` parameter. The hello-world container prints its message and then immediately exits (we redirected the output to `/dev/null` to keep the example output short). Next, we listed the containers again, as we saw that the hello-world container's read/write data was automatically removed when the container exited. After that, we ran the hello-world container again, but this time did not use the `--rm` parameter. When we listed the containers this time, we saw the indication of the (exited) container. Often you will run a container, knowing that you will never need to restart it later, and using the `--rm` parameter to automatically clean it up is very handy. But what if you don't use the `--rm` parameter? Are you stuck with an ever-growing list of containers? Of course not. Docker has a command for that. It is the `container rm` command.

The remove container command

The remove container command looks something like this:

```
# the new syntax
# Usage: docker container rm [OPTIONS] CONTAINER [CONTAINER...]
docker container rm cd828234194a

# the old syntax
docker rm cd828234194a
```

The command requires a value that uniquely identifies a container; in this case, I used the full container ID for the hello-world container that we just ran. You can use the first few characters of a container's ID, as long as it provides a unique identifier between all of the containers on your system. Another way to uniquely identify the container is by the name assigned to it. Docker will provide a unique randomly-generated name for your container when you run it. In the preceding example, the random name assigned was competent_payne. So we could have used the remove command like this:

```
# using the randomly generated name
docker container rm competent_payne
```

While the randomly-generated names provided by docker are more human-readable than the container IDs it assigns, they still may not be as relevant as you would like. This is why docker has provided an optional parameter to the run command for naming your containers. Here is an example using the --name parameter:

```
# using our own name
docker container run --name hi-earl hello-world
```

Now when we list all of the containers, we can see our container has the name hi-earl. Of course, you would probably want to use a better container name, perhaps one that describes the function performed by the container, such as db-for-earls-app.

Note: Like the container IDs, the container names must be unique on a host. You cannot have two containers (even if one has exited) that have the same name. If you will have more than one container running the same image, such as web server image, name them uniquely, for example, web01 and web02.

```
→ repos docker container run --name hi-earl hello-world > /dev/null
→ repos docker container ls -a
CONTAINER ID    IMAGE         COMMAND        CREATED         STATUS                    PORTS       NAMES
3f6c02d035e7    hello-world   "/hello"       23 seconds ago  Exited (0) 22 seconds ago             hi-earl
→ repos docker container run --name hi-earl hello-world > /dev/null
docker: Error response from daemon: Conflict. The container name "/hi-earl" is already in use by container "3f6c02d035e7f49e475fe77549889b8fa2eb6f88c3bc92753bcd
2adf7accc64b". You have to remove (or rename) that container to be able to reuse that name.
See 'docker run --help'.
→ repos docker container run --name hi-earl2 hello-world > /dev/null
→ repos docker container ls -a
CONTAINER ID    IMAGE         COMMAND        CREATED         STATUS                   PORTS       NAMES
55bfe831ec37    hello-world   "/hello"       4 seconds ago   Exited (0) 3 seconds ago              hi-earl2
3f6c02d035e7    hello-world   "/hello"       42 seconds ago  Exited (0) 41 seconds ago             hi-earl
→ repos ▊
```

You can delete multiple containers at the same time by providing the unique identifier for each on the command line:

```
# removing more than one
docker container rm hi-earl hi-earl2
```

Usually, you will remove containers only after they have exited, such as the hello-world containers that we have been using. However, sometimes you will want to remove a container even if it is currently running. You can use the `--force` parameter to handle that situation. Here is an example of using the force parameter to remove a running container:

```
# removing even if it is running
docker container rm --force web-server
```

Here is what that would look like:

```
→ repos docker container ls
CONTAINER ID     IMAGE          COMMAND              CREATED         STATUS         PORTS                    NAMES
155b95429337     nginx          "nginx -g 'daemon of…"   37 seconds ago    Up 36 seconds    0.0.0.0:80->80/tcp     web-server
→ repos docker container rm web-server
Error response from daemon: You cannot remove a running container 155b9542933786c1953caa3d23003f832dea2b8a6607c9d698079ed85a1b2a2a. Stop the
container before attempting removal or force remove
→ repos docker container rm --force web-server
web-server
→ repos docker container ls -a
CONTAINER ID     IMAGE          COMMAND              CREATED         STATUS         PORTS                    NAMES
→ repos ▊
```

Notice that in the first `container ls` command, we didn't use the `--all` parameter. This reminds us that the web server container is running. When we tried to remove it, we were informed that the container is still running and would not be removed. This is a good safeguard to help prevent the removal of running containers. Next, we used the force command, and the running container was removed without any warning. Finally, we did another `container ls` command, including the `--all` parameter to show that the read/write data for our container was actually removed this time.

> If you have set up Docker command completion, you can type in the command up to where you need to enter the unique identifier for the container(s) and then use the *Tab* key to get a list of containers, tabbing to the one you want to delete. Once you've highlighted the container to delete, use the space or *Enter* key to select it. You can hit *Tab* again to select another container to delete more than one at a time. Once you have all the containers selected, press *Enter* to execute the command. Remember that you will only see stopped containers when you tab for the `rm` command unless you include the force parameter, `rm -f`.

Sometimes, you may want to remove all of the containers on your system, running or not. There is a useful way to handle that situation. You can combine the `container ls` command and the container remove command to get the job done. You will be using a new parameter on the `container ls` command to accomplish this—the `--quiet` parameter. This command instructs Docker to only return the container IDs instead of the full list with a header. Here is the command:

```
# list just the container IDs
docker container ls --all --quiet
```

Now we can *feed* the values returned by the `container ls` command as input parameters to the container remove command. It will look like this:

```
# using full parameter names
docker container rm --force $(docker container ls --all --quiet)
# using short parameter names
docker container rm -f $(docker container ls -aq)

# using the old syntax
docker rm -f $(docker ps -aq)
```

This will remove *all* of the containers *both running and exited* from your system, so be careful!

> You will probably use this shortcut often, so creating a system alias for it is pretty handy.
> You can add something like the following to your `~/.bash_profile` or `~/zshrc` file: `alias RMAC='docker container rm --force $(docker container ls --all --quiet)'`.

Many containers are designed to run and exit immediately, such as the hello-world example we've used several times already. Other container's images are created so that, when you run a container using it, the container will continue running, providing some ongoing useful function, such as serving web pages. When you run a container that persists, it will hold onto the foreground process until it exits, attaching to the processes: standard input, standard output, and standard error. This is okay for some testing and development use cases, but normally, this would not be desired for a production container. Instead, it would be better to have the `container run` as a background process, giving you back control of your terminal session once it launches. Of course, there is a parameter for that. It is the `--detach` parameter. Here is what using that parameter looks like:

```
# using the full form of the parameter
docker container run --detach --name web-server --rm nginx
# using the short form of the parameter
docker container run -d --name web-server --rm nginx
```

Using this parameter detaches the process from the foreground session and returns control to you as soon as the container has started. Your next question is probably, how do I stop a detached container? Well, I am glad you asked. You use the `container stop` command.

The stop container command

The stop command is easy to use. Here are the syntax and an example of the command:

```
# Usage: docker container stop [OPTIONS] CONTAINER [CONTAINER...]
docker container stop web-server
```

In our case, we used the `--rm` parameter when running the container, so as soon as the container is stopped, the read/write layer will be automatically deleted. Like many of the Docker commands, you can provide more than one unique container identifier as parameters to stop more than one container with a single command.

Now you might be wondering if I use the `--detach` parameter, how do I see what is happening with the container? There are several ways you can get information from, and about, the container. Let's take a look at some of them before we continue with our run parameter exploration.

The container logs command

When you run a container in the foreground, all of the output the container sends to standard output and standard error is displayed in the console for the session that ran the container. However, when you use the `--detach` parameter, control of the session is returned as soon as the container starts so you don't see the data sent to `stdout` and `stderr`. If you want to see that data, you use the `container logs` command. That command looks like this:

```
# the long form of the command
# Usage: docker container logs [OPTIONS] CONTAINER
docker container logs --follow --timestamps web-server
# the short form of the command
docker container logs -f -t web-server

# get just the last 5 lines (there is no short form for the "--tail"
parameter)
docker container logs --tail 5 web-server

# the old syntax
docker logs web-server
```

The `--details`, `--follow`, `--timestamps`, and `--tail` parameters are all optional, but I have included them here for reference. When you use the `container logs` command with no optional parameters, it will just dump all of the contents of the container's logs to the console. You can use the `--tail` parameter with a number to dump just the last number of lines. You can combine the parameters (except for `--tail` and `--follow`) to get the results you want. The `--follow` parameter is like using a `tail -f` command when viewing logs that are being continually written to, and will display each line as it is written to the log. You use *Ctrl + C* to exit the log being followed. The `--timestamps` parameter is great for evaluating the frequency at which lines have been written to the container's logs.

The container top command

You may not always want to simply view the logs of a container; sometimes you want to know what processes are running inside a container. That's where the `container top` command comes in. Ideally, each container is running a single process, but the world is not always ideal, so you can use a command such as this to view all the processes running in the targeted container:

```
# using the new syntax
# Usage: docker container top CONTAINER [ps OPTIONS]
docker container top web-server

# using the old syntax
docker top web-server
```

As you might expect, the `container top` command is only used for viewing the processes of a single container at a time.

The container inspect command

When you run a container, there is a lot of metadata that gets associated with the container. There are many times that you will want to review that metadata. The command for doing that is:

```
# using the new syntax
# Usage: docker container inspect [OPTIONS] CONTAINER [CONTAINER...]
docker container inspect web-server

# using the old syntax
docker inspect web-server
```

As mentioned, this command returns a lot of data. You may only be interested in a subset of the metadata. You can use the `--format` parameter to narrow the data returned. Check out these examples:

- Getting some State data:

```
# if you want to see the state of a container you can use this command
docker container inspect --format '{{json .State}}' web-server1 | jq
```

```
# if you want to narrow the state data to just when the container started,
use this command
docker container inspect --format '{{json .State}}' web-server1 | jq
'.StartedAt'
```

- Getting some `NetworkSettings` data:

```
# if you are interested in the container's network settings, use this
command
docker container inspect --format '{{json .NetworkSettings}}' web-server1 |
jq
```

```
# or maybe you just want to see the ports used by the container, here is a
command for that
docker container inspect --format '{{json .NetworkSettings}}' web-server1 |
jq '.Ports'
```

```
# maybe you just want the IP address used by the container, this is the
command you could use.
docker container inspect -f '{{json .NetworkSettings}}' web-server1 | jq
'.IPAddress'
```

- Getting data for more than one container with a single command:

```
# maybe you want the IP Addresses for a couple containers
docker container inspect -f '{{json .NetworkSettings}}' web-server1 web-
server2 | jq '.IPAddress'
```

```
# since the output for each container is a single line, this one can be
done without using jq
docker container inspect -f '{{ .NetworkSettings.IPAddress }}' web-server1
web-server2 web-server3
```

Most of these examples use the json processor, `jq`. If you haven't already installed it on your system, now is a good time to do so. Here are the commands to install `jq` on each of the OSes we've used in this book:

```
# install jq on Mac OS
brew install jq

# install jq on ubuntu
sudo apt-get install jq

# install jq on RHEL/CentOS
yum install -y epel-release
yum install -y jq

# install jq on Windows using Chocolatey NuGet package manager
chocolatey install jq
```

The `--format` parameter of the inspect command uses go templates. You can find more information about them on the Docker document pages for formatting output: `https://docs.docker.com/config/formatting`.

The container stats command

Another very useful Docker command is the stats command. It provides live, continually-updated usage statistics for one or more running containers. It is a bit like using the Linux `top` command. You can run the command with no parameters to view the stats for all running containers, or you can provide one or more unique container identifiers to view the stats for one or more container's specific containers. Here are some examples of using the command:

```
# using the new syntax, view the stats for all running containers
# Usage: docker container stats [OPTIONS] [CONTAINER...]
docker container stats

# view the stats for just two web server containers
docker container stats web-server1 web-server2

# using the old syntax, view stats for all running containers
docker stats
```

When you have seen enough stats, you use *Ctrl* + *C* to exit the view.

Getting back to `run` command parameters, next, we'll discuss two parameters for the `run` command that are usually used together. Sometimes you run a container, and you want to have an interactive session with it. For example, you may run a container that executes some application inside a more or less full OS, such as Ubuntu, and you want to have access inside that container to change the configuration or debug some issue, similar to using SSH to connect to a server. As with most things Docker, there is more than one way to accomplish this. One common method is to use two optional parameters for the run command: `--interactive` and `--tty`. Let's take a look at how that works now. You have already seen how we can use the `--detach` parameter startup disconnected from the container we are running:

```
# running detached
docker container run --detach --name web-server1 nginx
```

When we run this command to start up our nginx web server and browse to `http://localhost`, we find that it is not serving the welcome page we expect. So we decide to do some debugging, and, instead of detaching from our container, we decide to run it interactively using the two `--interactive` and `--tty` parameters. Now, since this is a nginx container, it has a default command that is executed when the container starts. That command is `nginx -g 'daemon off;'`. Since that is the default command, it won't do us any good to interact with the container. So we are going to override the default command by providing one as a parameter to our run command. It will look something like this:

```
# using the long form of the parameters
docker container run --interactive --tty --name web-server2 nginx bash
```

```
# using the short form of the parameters (joined as one), which is much
more common usage
docker container run -it --name web-server2 nginx bash
```

This command will run the container as before, but instead of executing the default command, it will execute the `bash` command. It will also open a terminal session with the container that we can interact with. As needed, we can execute commands inside of the container as the `root` user. We can view folders and files, we can edit configuration settings, we can install packages, and so on. We can even run the image's default command to see whether we have resolved any issues. Here is a somewhat contrived example:

```
→ repos docker container run --interactive --tty --name web-server2 -p 80:80 nginx bash
root@fe7aebfe712f:/# ls /etc/nginx
conf.d  fastcgi_params  koi-utf  koi-win  mime.types  modules  nginx.conf  scgi_params  uwsgi_params  win-utf
root@fe7aebfe712f:/# cat /etc/nginx/conf.d/default.conf |grep server_name
    server_name  localhost;
root@fe7aebfe712f:/# cat /etc/nginx/conf.d/default.conf |grep "listen "
    listen       80;
root@fe7aebfe712f:/# #looks good, running on localhost:80, lets start the default CMD
root@fe7aebfe712f:/# nginx
root@fe7aebfe712f:/# 172.17.0.1 - - [15/Jul/2018:22:06:09 +0000] "GET / HTTP/1.1" 304 0 "-" "Mozilla/5.0 (Macintosh;
L, like Gecko) Chrome/65.0.3325.183 Safari/537.36 Vivaldi/1.96.1147.52" "-"
^C
root@fe7aebfe712f:/# exit
exit
→ repos
```

You may have noticed the `-p 80:80` parameter. That is the short form of the publish parameter, which we will discuss shortly in the *Back to the Docker run command* section. Using the `container ls` command, you can see the differences between running the container using the default command versus running the container using an override command:

```
→ repos docker container run --detach --name web-server1 -p 80:80 nginx
c441a1db4f171fa7fa54c8f90ff9316204c6d70e241ad49c7365da87db3036f3
→ repos docker container run --interactive --tty --name web-server2 -p 8080:80 nginx bash
root@00a2ab03e7bc:/# exit
exit
→ repos docker container ls --all
CONTAINER ID    IMAGE    COMMAND                 CREATED          STATUS                      PORTS                   NAMES
00a2ab03e7bc    nginx    "bash"                  15 seconds ago   Exited (0) 10 seconds ago                           web-server2
c441a1db4f17    nginx    "nginx -g 'daemon of…"  25 seconds ago   Up 25 seconds               0.0.0.0:80->80/tcp      web-server1
→ repos ▮
```

Web-server run used the default CMD, and web-server2 used the override CMD `bash`. This is a contrived example to help you understand these concepts. A real-world example might be when you want to interactively connect with an OS-based container, such as Ubuntu. You may recall that at the beginning of Chapter 1, *Setting up a Docker Development Environment*, it said that the default command run in an Ubuntu container is `bash`. Since that is the case, you don't have to supply a command to override the default. You can use a run command like this:

```
# running interactively with default CMD
docker container run -it --name earls-dev ubuntu
```

With this `container run` command, you are connected to an interactive terminal session of your running Ubuntu container. You can do pretty much anything you would normally do when ssh-ed into an Ubuntu server. You can install software with `apt-get`, you can view running processes, you can execute a `top` command, and so on. That might look like this:

```
→ repos docker container run -it --name earls-dev ubuntu
root@f347b57a978b:/# cat /etc/debian_version
buster/sid
root@f347b57a978b:/# curl google.com
bash: curl: command not found
root@f347b57a978b:/# apt-get update > /dev/null
root@f347b57a978b:/# apt-get install -y curl > /dev/null
debconf: delaying package configuration, since apt-utils is not installed
root@f347b57a978b:/# curl google.com
<HTML><HEAD><meta http-equiv="content-type" content="text/html;charset=utf-8">
<TITLE>301 Moved</TITLE></HEAD><BODY>
<H1>301 Moved</H1>
The document has moved
<A HREF="http://www.google.com/">here</A>.
</BODY></HTML>
root@f347b57a978b:/# exit
exit
→ repos ▊
```

There are a couple of other container commands that help you interact with a container that is already running and is detached. Let's take a quick look at these commands now.

The container attach command

Suppose you have a running container. It is currently detached from your terminal session. You can use the `container attach` command to bring that container's executing process to be the foreground process of your terminal session. Let's use the web-server example we used earlier:

```
# run a container detached
docker container run --detach -it --name web-server1 -p 80:80 nginx

# show that the container is running
docker container ps

# attach to the container
# Usage: docker container attach [OPTIONS] CONTAINER
docker container attach web-server1
```

```
# issue a Ctrl + PQ keystroke to detach (except for Docker on Mac, see
below for special Mac instructions)

# again, show that the container is running detached.
docker container ps
```

When you attach to the running container, its executing command becomes the foreground process for your terminal session. To detach from the container, you need to issue a *Ctrl + PQ* keystroke. If you issue a *Ctrl + C* keystroke, the container's executing process will receive a sig-term signal and will terminate, which in turn will exit the container. This is usually not desired. So remember to detach by using a *Ctrl + PQ* keystroke.

However, there is a known issue on macOS: for Docker on Mac, the *Ctrl + PQ* keystroke does not work, and unless you use another parameter, the `--sig-proxy=false` parameter, on the `attach` command, you will not be able to detach from the container without terminating it with a *Ctrl + C* keystroke:

```
# when you are using Docker for Mac, remember to always add the "--sig-
proxy=false" parameter
docker attach --sig-proxy=false web-server1
```

When you provide the `--sig-proxy=false` parameter to the `attach` command, you can issue a *Ctrl + C* keystroke to the attached container and it will detach without sending the sig-term signal to the container process, thus keeping the container running, once again detached from your terminal session:

```
→ repos docker container run --detach --name web-server1 -p 80:80 nginx
4d20cb0f4a2c91924f74713a8881f772832cba2566070941a885407c331b834c
→ repos docker ps
CONTAINER ID     IMAGE          COMMAND              CREATED        STATUS         PORTS                  NAMES
4d20cb0f4a2c     nginx          "nginx -g 'daemon of…"  5 seconds ago  Up 6 seconds   0.0.0.0:80->80/tcp     web-server1
→ repos docker container attach --sig-proxy=false web-server1
172.17.0.1 - - [15/Jul/2018:23:15:24 +0000] "GET / HTTP/1.1" 304 0 "-" "Mozilla/5.0 (Macintosh; Intel Mac OS X 10_12_0) AppleWebKit/537.36
/65.0.3325.183 Safari/537.36 Vivaldi/1.96.1147.52" "-"
172.17.0.1 - - [15/Jul/2018:23:15:24 +0000] "GET / HTTP/1.1" 304 0 "-" "Mozilla/5.0 (Macintosh; Intel Mac OS X 10_12_0) AppleWebKit/537.36
/65.0.3325.183 Safari/537.36 Vivaldi/1.96.1147.52" "-"
^C
→ repos docker ps
CONTAINER ID     IMAGE          COMMAND              CREATED         STATUS          PORTS                  NAMES
4d20cb0f4a2c     nginx          "nginx -g 'daemon of…"  33 seconds ago  Up 34 seconds   0.0.0.0:80->80/tcp     web-server1
→ repos
```

The container exec command

Sometimes, when you have a container running detached, you might want to get access to it, but don't want to attach to the executing command. You can accomplish this by using the container exec command. This command allows you to execute another command in the running container, without attaching to or interfering with the already-running command. This command is often used to create an interactive session with an already-running container or to execute a single command within the container. The command looks like this:

```
# start an nginx container detached
docker container run --detach --name web-server1 -p 80:80 nginx

# see that the container is currently running
docker container ls

# execute other commands in the running container
# Usage: docker container exec [OPTIONS] CONTAINER COMMAND [ARG...]
docker container exec -it web-server1 bash
docker container exec web-server1 cat /etc/debian_version

# confirm that the container is still running
docker container ls
```

When the exec command completes, you exit the bash shell, or the file contents have been displaced, then it exits back to the terminal session leaving the container running detached:

```
→ repos RMAC
47cecd4dc391
→ repos docker container run --detach --name web-server1 -p 80:80 nginx
0cb95633c51285b02ec33912c2f6d7c2ad7dd156ec06f074ddf30dd45b8549d7
→ repos docker container ls
CONTAINER ID    IMAGE        COMMAND              CREATED         STATUS           PORTS                  NAMES
0cb95633c512    nginx        "nginx -g 'daemon of…"  5 seconds ago   Up 4 seconds     0.0.0.0:80->80/tcp     web-server1
→ repos docker container exec -it web-server1 bash
root@0cb95633c512:/# apt-get update > /dev/null
root@0cb95633c512:/# apt-get install -y curl > /dev/null
debconf: delaying package configuration, since apt-utils is not installed
root@0cb95633c512:/# exit
exit
→ repos docker container exec web-server1 cat /etc/debian_version
9.4
→ repos docker container ls
CONTAINER ID    IMAGE        COMMAND              CREATED          STATUS           PORTS                  NAMES
0cb95633c512    nginx        "nginx -g 'daemon of…"  About a minute ago  Up About a minute  0.0.0.0:80->80/tcp     web-server1
→ repos █
```

Let's take a look at another Docker command before we continue our discussion of the many optional container run parameters.

The container commit command

It is important to know that when you are attached to a running container and make changes to it, such as installing new packages, or changing configuration files, that those changes only apply to that running container. If, for example, you use an Ubuntu image to run a container and then install `curl` into that container, the change does not apply back to the image you ran the container from, in this example, Ubuntu. If you were to start another container from the same Ubuntu image, you would need to install `curl` again. However, if you want to have the changes you make inside a running container persist and be available when you run new containers, you can use the `container commit` command. The `container commit` command allows you to save the current read/write layer of a container along with the layers of the original image, creating a brand new image. When you run containers using the new image, it will include the changes you made and saved with the `container commit` command. Here is what the `container commit` command looks like:

```
# Usage: docker container commit [OPTIONS] CONTAINER [REPOSITORY[:TAG]]
docker container commit ubuntu new-ubuntu
```

And here is an example of using the `container commit` command to install `curl` to a running container, and then creating a new container that includes the installed `curl` command:

```
→ repos docker images
REPOSITORY          TAG           IMAGE ID          CREATED         SIZE
hello-world         latest        2cb0d9787c4d      5 days ago      1.85kB
nginx               latest        3c5a05123222      9 days ago      109MB
ubuntu              latest        113a43faa138      5 weeks ago     81.2MB
→ repos docker container run -it --name ubuntu ubuntu
root@438040ea1218:/# curl google.com
bash: curl: command not found
root@438040ea1218:/# apt-get update > /dev/null
root@438040ea1218:/# apt-get install -y curl > /dev/null
debconf: delaying package configuration, since apt-utils is not installed
root@438040ea1218:/# curl google.com
<HTML><HEAD><meta http-equiv="content-type" content="text/html;charset=utf-8">
<TITLE>301 Moved</TITLE></HEAD><BODY>
<H1>301 Moved</H1>
The document has moved
<A HREF="http://www.google.com/">here</A>.
</BODY></HTML>
root@438040ea1218:/# exit
exit
→ repos docker container ls -a
CONTAINER ID    IMAGE        COMMAND         CREATED           STATUS                  PORTS       NAMES
438040ea1218    ubuntu       "/bin/bash"     About a minute ago  Exited (0) 10 seconds ago         ubuntu
→ repos docker container commit ubuntu new-ubuntu
sha256:99248b85956d939ed71785c78c46d1845717dceac7d7fb2df6178161e42fd200
→ repos docker images
REPOSITORY          TAG           IMAGE ID          CREATED         SIZE
new-ubuntu          latest        99248b85956d      3 seconds ago   136MB
hello-world         latest        2cb0d9787c4d      5 days ago      1.85kB
nginx               latest        3c5a05123222      9 days ago      109MB
ubuntu              latest        113a43faa138      5 weeks ago     81.2MB
→ repos docker container run -it --name earls-dev new-ubuntu
root@00acf2607da86:/# curl google.com
<HTML><HEAD><meta http-equiv="content-type" content="text/html;charset=utf-8">
<TITLE>301 Moved</TITLE></HEAD><BODY>
<H1>301 Moved</H1>
The document has moved
<A HREF="http://www.google.com/">here</A>.
</BODY></HTML>
root@00acf2607da86:/# exit
exit
→ repos █
```

With this example, I can now run new containers from the ubuntu-curl image, and all of them will have the curl command already installed.

Back to the Docker run command

Now, let's return to our discussion of the container run command. Earlier, you saw an example of using the run command with the --publish parameter. Using the optional publish parameter allows you to specify what ports will be opened related to the run container. The --publish parameter includes pairs of port numbers separated by a colon. For example:

```
# create an nginx web-server that redirects host traffic from port 8080 to
port 80 in the container
docker container run --detach --name web-server1 --publish 8080:80 nginx
```

The first port number is associated with the host running the container. In the nginx example, `8080` is exposed on the host; in our case that would be `http://localhost:8080`. The second port number is the port that is open on the running container. In this case, it would be `80`. Speaking out the description of the `--publish` `8080:80` parameter, you would say something like, the traffic sent to port `8080` on the host is redirected to port `80` on the running container:

It is an important distinction to make between the host ports and the container ports. I can run several containers on the same system that all expose port `80`, but only one container can have traffic from each port on the host. Look at the following examples to better understand:

```
# all of these can be running at the same time
docker container run --detach --name web-server1 --publish 80:80 nginx
docker container run --detach --name web-server2 --publish 8000:80 nginx
docker container run --detach --name web-server3 --publish 8080:80 nginx
docker container run --detach --name web-server4 --publish 8888:80 nginx

# however if you tried to run this one too, it would fail to run
# because the host already has port 80 assigned to web-server1
docker container run --detach --name web-server5 --publish 80:80 nginx
```

Know that this is a limitation of networking in general, not a limitation of Docker or containers. Here we can see these commands and their output. Notice the ports and names, and how the use of a port already used as an endpoint fails:

```
→ repos docker container run --detach --name web-server1 --publish 80:80 nginx
48b58f6b8bd0ea970a76be913a1162d66221965ac836e75afdbe6c1eb76b71ef
→ repos docker container run --detach --name web-server2 --publish 8000:80 nginx
4c783d0e75d6cda48a8086f5906182f1b092fa7f98f42c134549d10646dc72af
→ repos docker container run --detach --name web-server3 --publish 8080:80 nginx
eb0bb723ad6e65f305584790ac3dc14046437f1df2b0cb315aa5329a21d1b7e9c
→ repos docker container run --detach --name web-server4 --publish 8888:80 nginx
71d24f4df17e031fe20c93f7beff0b581bc66b43ea2e7c7ad8395cd5c188
→ repos docker container ls
CONTAINER ID   IMAGE    COMMAND               CREATED          STATUS          PORTS                    NAMES
71d24f4df17e   nginx    "nginx -g 'daemon of…"  6 seconds ago    Up 5 seconds    0.0.0.0:8888->80/tcp     web-server4
eb0bb723ad6e   nginx    "nginx -g 'daemon of…"  14 seconds ago   Up 13 seconds   0.0.0.0:8080->80/tcp     web-server3
4c783d0e75d6   nginx    "nginx -g 'daemon of…"  23 seconds ago   Up 23 seconds   0.0.0.0:8000->80/tcp     web-server2
48b58f6b8bd0   nginx    "nginx -g 'daemon of…"  37 seconds ago   Up 36 seconds   0.0.0.0:80->80/tcp       web-server1
→ repos docker container run --detach --name web-server5 --publish 80:80 nginx
81add1ae1960da1879d604fa060341dbce5c94248a587d205cd446b88d87be3c
docker: Error response from daemon: driver failed programming external connectivity on endpoint web-server5 (2da7468fc28388414bd13a1180b229
be75b002ac8eef5937b5dcb7ab04dc0c3e): Bind for 0.0.0.0:80 failed: port is already allocated.
→ repos
```

That was a lot of data on various options parameters for the `container run` command. It's not all the options parameters, but it should be enough to get you off to a great start. If you want to learn more about the optional parameters we explored, or find out about the ones we didn't cover here, be sure to visit the docker documents page for the `container run` command, which can be found at `https://docs.docker.com/engine/reference/run/`.

Summary

In this chapter, we learned about Docker image descriptions and a little about Docker registries. Then we saw that there is another form of the version command. After that, we explored a lot of Docker container commands, including `run`, `stop`, `ls`, `logs`, `top`, `stats`, `attach`, `exec`, and the `commit` command. Finally, we found out how to expose your containers by opening ports from your host and to your containers. You should feel pretty good about what you can do with Docker already, but hang on—in Chapter 3, *Creating Docker Images*, we are going to show you how to create your own Docker images with a `Dockerfile` and the image build command. If you're ready, turn the page.

References

- Docker registry: `https://hub.docker.com/explore/`
- All of the parameters for the `container run` command: `https://docs.docker.com/engine/reference/run/`
- Using the `--format` parameter with the container inspect command: `https://docs.docker.com/config/formatting`
- The json jq parser: `https://stedolan.github.io/jq/`
- The Chocolatey Windows package manager: `https://chocolatey.org/`

3
Creating Docker Images

In this chapter, we will learn how to create enterprise-grade Docker images. We will start off by learning about the main building block of Docker images, specifically the Dockerfile. Then, we will explore all the instructions available to use in a Dockerfile. There are some instructions that on the surface seem very similar. We will uncover what the differences are between the COPY and ADD instructions, the ENV and ARG instructions, and most importantly between the CMD and ENTRYPOINT instructions. Next, we will find out what the build context is and why it is important. Finally, we will cover the actual image build command.

> *If well-maintained, the average shipping container has a lifespan of around 20 years, whereas the average lifespan of a Docker container is 2.5 days.*

```
–https://www.tintri.com/blog/2017/03/tintri-supports-containers-advanced-
storage-features
```

In this chapter, we will cover the following topics:

- What is a Dockerfile?
- All of the instructions that can be used in a Dockerfile
- When to use either the COPY or the ADD instruction
- The difference between the ENV and ARG variables
- Why you use the CMD and ENTRYPOINT instructions
- The importance of the build context
- Building Docker images using a Dockerfile

Technical requirements

You will be pulling Docker images from Docker's public repository, so basic internet access is required to execute the examples within this chapter.

The code files of this chapter can be found on GitHub:

```
https://github.com/PacktPublishing/Docker-Quick-Start-Guide/tree/master/
Chapter03
```

Check out the following video to see the code in action:
```
http://bit.ly/2rbHvwC
```

What is a Dockerfile?

You learned in `Chapter 2`, *Learning Docker Commands*, that you can run a Docker container, make modifications to that running container, and then using the docker commit command, save those changes, effectively creating a new Docker image. Although this method works, it is not the preferred way to create Docker containers. The best way to create Docker images is to use the Docker image build command with a Dockerfile that describes your desired image.

A Dockerfile (yes, the correct spelling is all one word, with a capital *D*) is a text file that contains instructions used by the Docker daemon to create a Docker image. The instructions are defined using a type of value pair syntax. Each one has an instruction word followed by the parameters for that instruction. Every command gets its own line in the Dockerfile. Although the Dockerfile instructions are not case-sensitive, there is a well-used convention that the instruction word is always uppercase.

The order of the instructions in the Dockerfile is significant. Instructions are evaluated in sequential order, starting at the top of the Dockerfile and finishing at the bottom of the file. If you recall from `Chapter 1`, *Setting up a Docker Development Environment*, Docker images are made up of layers. All of the instructions found in the Dockerfile will result in a new layer being generated as the Docker image is built, however, some instructions will only add a zero-byte-sized metadata layer to the created image. Since it is a best practice to keep Docker images as small as possible, you will want to use instructions that create non-zero-byte-sized layers as efficiently as possible. In the following sections, we'll note where using an instruction creates a non-zero-byte-sized layer, and how to best use that instruction to minimize the number and size of layers. Another important consideration is the ordering of the instructions. Certain instructions must be used before others, but with those exceptions, you can place the other instructions in any order you please. The best practice is to use instructions that change least early in the Dockerfile, and instructions that change more frequently in the later part of the Dockerfile. The reason is that when you need to rebuild an image, the only layers that get rebuilt are the ones that are at, or after, the first line changed in the Dockerfile. If you don't understand this yet, don't worry, it will make more sense once we see some examples.

We will review the build command at the end of this section, but we will start with the instructions available to the Dockerfile first, beginning with the instruction that has to be the first instruction in your Dockerfile: the FROM instruction.

The FROM instruction

Every Dockerfile must have a FROM instruction, and it must be the first instruction in the file. (Actually, the ARG instruction can be used before a FROM instruction, but it is not a required instruction. We will talk more about that in the ARG instruction section.)

The FROM instruction sets the base for the image being created and instructs the Docker daemon that the base of the new image should be the existing Docker image specified as the parameter. The specified image can be described using the same syntax we saw in the Docker container run command from Chapter 2, *Learning Docker Commands*. Here, it's a FROM instruction that specifies using the official nginx image with a version of 1.15.2:

```
# Dockerfile
FROM nginx:1.15.2
```

Note that in this example, there is no repository specified that indicates that the specified image is the official nginx image. If no tag is specified, the latest tag will be assumed.

The FROM instruction will create the first layer in our new image. That layer will be the size of the image specified in the instruction's parameter so it is best to specify the smallest image that meets the criteria needed for your new image. An application-specific image, such as nginx, is going to be smaller than an OS image, such as ubuntu. And, the OS image for alpine will be much smaller than images of other OSes, such as Ubuntu, CentOS, or RHEL. There is a special keyword that can be used as the parameter to the FROM instruction. It is scratch. Scratch is not an image that you can pull or run, it just a signal to the Docker daemon that you want to build an image with an empty base-image layer. The FROM scratch instruction is used as the base layer for many other base images, or for specialized app-specific images. You have already seen an example of such a specialized app image: hello-world. The full Dockerfile for the hello-world image looks like this:

```
# hello-world Dockerfile
FROM scratch
COPY hello /
CMD ["/hello"]
```

We will discuss the COPY and CMD instructions shortly, but you should get a sense of how small the hello-world image is based on its Dockerfile. In the world of Docker images, smaller is definitely better. Take a look at the size of some images for reference:

```
→ hello-earl docker image ls
REPOSITORY        TAG        IMAGE ID         CREATED         SIZE
hello-earl        1.0.0      36ca4bf4a79f     5 minutes ago   1.85kB
ubuntu            latest     735f80812f90     8 days ago      83.5MB
nginx             alpine     36f3464a2197     10 days ago     18.6MB
nginx             latest     c82521676580     10 days ago     109MB
hello-world       latest     2cb0d9787c4d     3 weeks ago     1.85kB
alpine            latest     11cd0b38bc3c     4 weeks ago     4.41MB
```

The LABEL instruction

The LABEL instruction is a way to add metadata to your Docker image. This instruction adds embedded key-value pairs to the image. The LABEL instruction adds a zero-byte-sized layer to the image when it is created. An image can have more than one LABEL, and each LABEL instruction can provide one or more LABELs. The most common use for the LABEL instruction is to provide information about the image maintainer. This data used to have its own instruction. See the following tip box about the now-deprecated MAINTAINER instruction. Here are some examples of valid LABEL instructions:

```
# LABEL instruction syntax
# LABEL <key>=<value> <key>=<value> <key>=<value> ...
LABEL maintainer="Earl Waud <earlwaud@mycompany.com>"
LABEL "description"="My development Ubuntu image"
LABEL version="1.0"
LABEL label1="value1" \
 label2="value2" \
 lable3="value3"
LABEL my-multi-line-label="Labels can span \
more than one line in a Dockerfile."
LABEL support-email="support@mycompany.com" support-phone=" (123) 456-7890"
```

The LABEL instruction is one of the instructions that can be used multiple times in a Dockerfile. You will learn later that some instructions that can be used multiple times will result in only the last use being significant, thus ignoring all previous uses. The LABEL instruction is different. Every use of the LABEL instruction adds an additional label to the resulting image. However, if two or more uses of LABEL have the same key, the label will get the value provided in the last matching LABEL instruction. That looks like this:

```
# earlier in the Dockerfile
LABEL version="1.0"
# later in the Dockerfile...
LABEL version="2.0"
# The Docker image metadata will show version="2.0"
```

It is important to know that the base image specified in your FROM instruction may include labels created with the LABEL instruction and that they will automatically be included in the metadata of the image you are building. If a LABEL instruction in your Dockerfile uses the same key as a LABEL instruction used in the FROM image's Dockerfile, your (later) value will override the one in the FROM image. You can view all of the labels for an image by using the inspect command:

```
➜ hello-earl docker image inspect --format '{{json .Config}}' hello-earl:1.0.1 | jq '.Labels'
{
    "description": "My development Ubuntu image",
    "label1": "value1",
    "label2": "value2",
    "lable3": "value3",
    "maintainer": "Earl Waud <earlwaud@mycompany.com>",
    "my-multi-line-label": "Labels can span more than one line in a Dockerfile.",
    "support-email": "support@mycompany.com",
    "support-phone": "(123) 456-7890",
    "version": "2.0"
}
```

The MAINTAINER instruction

There is a Dockerfile instruction specifically for providing the info about the image maintainer, however, this instruction has been deprecated. Still, you will probably see it used in a Dockerfile at some point. The syntax goes like this: "maintainer": "Earl Waud <earlwaud@mycompany.com>".

The COPY instruction

You have already seen an example of using the COPY instruction in the hello-world Dockerfile shown in *The FROM instruction* section. The COPY instruction is used to copy files and folders into the Docker image being built. The syntax for the COPY instruction is as follows:

```
# COPY instruction syntax
COPY [--chown=<user>:<group>] <src>... <dest>
# Use double quotes for paths containing whitespace)
COPY [--chown=<user>:<group>] ["<src>",... "<dest>"]
```

Note that the --chown parameter is only valid for Linux-based containers. Without the --chown parameter, the owner ID and group ID will both be set to 0.

The <src> or source is a filename or folder path and is interpreted to be relative to the context of the build. We will talk more about the build context later in this chapter, but for now, think of it as where the build command is run. The source may include wildcards.

The <dest> or destination is a filename or path inside of the image being created. The destination is relative to the root of the image's filesystem unless there is a preceding WORKDIR instruction. We will discuss the WORKDIR instruction later, but for now, just think of it as a way to set the current working directory. When the COPY command comes after a WORKDIR instruction in a Dockerfile, the file or folders being copied into the image will be placed in the destination relative to the current working directory. If the destination includes a path with one or more folders, all of the folders will be created if they don't already exist.

In our earlier hello-world Dockerfile example, you saw a COPY instruction that copied an executable file, named hello, into the image at the filesystem's root location. It looked like this: COPY hello /. That is about as basic a COPY instruction as can be used. Here are some other examples:

```
# COPY instruction Dockerfile for Docker Quick Start
FROM alpine:latest
LABEL maintainer="Earl Waud <earlwaud@mycompany.com>"
LABEL version=1.0
# copy multiple files, creating the path "/theqsg/files" in the process
COPY file* theqsg/files/
# copy all of the contents of folder "folder1" to "/theqsg/"
# (but not the folder "folder1" itself)
COPY folder1 theqsg/
# change the current working directory in the image to "/theqsg"
WORKDIR theqsg
```

```
# copy the file special1 into "/theqsg/special-files/"
COPY --chown=35:35 special1 special-files/
# return the current working directory to "/"
WORKDIR /
CMD ["sh"]
```

We can see what the resulting image's filesystem would get using the preceding Dockerfile by running a container from the image, and executing an `ls` command, which would look like this:

```
➜ qds-samples docker container run --rm copy-demo:1.0 ls -l -R theqsg
theqsg:
total 8
drwxr-xr-x    2 root     root        4096 Aug  4 03:27 files
-rw-r--r--    1 root     root           0 Aug  4 03:27 folderfile1
-rw-r--r--    1 root     root           0 Aug  4 03:27 folderfile2
drwxr-xr-x    2 games    games       4096 Aug  4 03:44 special-files

theqsg/files:
total 0
-rw-r--r--    1 root     root           0 Aug  4 03:26 file1
-rw-r--r--    1 root     root           0 Aug  4 03:26 file2
-rw-r--r--    1 root     root           0 Aug  4 03:26 file3

theqsg/special-files:
total 0
-rw-r--r--    1 games    games          0 Aug  4 03:27 special1
➜ qds-samples █
```

You can see that folders specified in the destination path were created during the COPY. You will also notice that providing the `--chown` parameter sets the owner and group on the destination files. An important distinction is that when the source is a folder, the contents of the folder are copied but not the folder itself. Notice that using a WORKDIR instruction changes the path in the image filesystem and following COPY instructions will now be relative to the new current working directory. In this example, we returned the current working directory to / so that commands executed in containers will run relative to /.

The ADD instruction

The ADD instruction is used to copy files and folders into the Docker image being built. The syntax for the ADD instruction is as follows:

```
# ADD instruction syntax
ADD [--chown=<user>:<group>] <src>... <dest>
# Use double quotes for paths containing whitespace)
ADD [--chown=<user>:<group>] ["<src>",... "<dest>"]
```

About now, you are thinking that the ADD instruction seems to be just like the COPY instruction that we just reviewed. Well, you are not wrong. Basically, all of the things we saw the COPY instruction do, the ADD instruction can do as well. It uses the same syntax as the COPY instruction and the effects of WORKDIR instructions are the same between the two. So, why do we have two commands that do the same thing?

The difference between COPY and ADD

The answer is that the ADD instruction can actually do more than the COPY instruction. The more is dependent upon the values used for the source input. With the COPY instruction, the source can be files or folders. However, with the ADD instruction, the source can be files, folders, a local .tar file, or a URL.

When the ADD instruction has a source value that is a .tar file, the contents of that TAR file are extracted into a corresponding folder inside the image.

When you use a .tar file as the source in an ADD instruction and include the --chown parameter, you might expect the owner and group in the image to be set on the files extracted from the archive. This is currently not the way it works. Unfortunately, the owner, group, and permissions on the extracted contents will match what is contained within the archive in spite of the --chown parameter. When you use a .tar file, you will probably want to include RUN chown -R X:X after the ADD.

As mentioned, the ADD instruction can use a URL as the source value. Here is an example Dockerfile that includes an ADD instruction using a URL:

```
# ADD instruction Dockerfile for Docker Quick Start
FROM alpine
LABEL maintainer="Earl Waud <earlwaud@mycompany.com>"
LABEL version=3.0
ADD
https://github.com/docker-library/hello-world/raw/master/amd64/hello-world/
hello /
RUN chmod +x /hello
CMD ["/hello"]
```

While using a URL in an ADD instruction works, downloading the file into the image, this feature is not recommended, even by Docker. Here is what the Docker documentation has to say about using ADD:

> Because image size matters, using ADD to fetch packages from remote URLs is strongly discouraged; you should use `curl` or `wget` instead. That way you can delete the files you no longer need after they've been extracted and you don't have to add another layer in your image. For example, you should avoid doing things like:
>
> ```
> ADD http://example.com/big.tar.xz /usr/src/things/
> RUN tar -xJf /usr/src/things/big.tar.xz -C /usr/src/things
> RUN make -C /usr/src/things all
> ```
>
> And instead, do something like:
>
> ```
> RUN mkdir -p /usr/src/things \
>     && curl -SL http://example.com/big.tar.xz \
>     | tar -xJC /usr/src/things \
>     && make -C /usr/src/things all
> ```
>
> For other items (files, directories) that do not require ADD 's tar auto-extraction capability, you should always use `COPY` .

So, generally speaking, whenever you can get the desired content into the image using a COPY instruction, then you should choose to use COPY instead of ADD.

The ENV instruction

As you may guess, the ENV instruction is used to define environment variables that will be set in the running containers created from the image being built. The variables are defined using typical key-value pairs. A Dockerfile can have one or more ENV instructions. Here is the ENV instruction syntax:

```
# ENV instruction syntax
# This is the form to create a single environment variable per instruction
# Everything after the space following the <key> becomes the value
ENV <key> <value>
# This is the form to use when you want to create more than one variable
per instruction
ENV <key>=<value> ...
```

Each ENV instruction will create one or more environment variables (unless the key name is repeated). Let's take a look at some ENV instructions in a Dockerfile:

```
# ENV instruction Dockerfile for Docker Quick Start
FROM alpine
LABEL maintainer="Earl Waud <earlwaud@mycompany.com>"
ENV appDescription This app is a sample of using ENV instructions
ENV appName=env-demo
ENV note1="The First Note First" note2=The\ Second\ Note\ Second \
note3="The Third Note Third"
ENV changeMe="Old Value"
CMD ["sh"]
```

After building the image using this Dockerfile, you can inspect the image metadata and see the environment variables that have been created:

```
→ dqs-samples git:(master) ✗ docker image inspect --format '{{json .Config}}' env-demo:1.0 | jq '.Env'
[
  "PATH=/usr/local/sbin:/usr/local/bin:/usr/sbin:/usr/bin:/sbin:/bin",
  "appDescription=This app is a sample of using ENV instructions",
  "appName=env-demo",
  "note1=The First Note First",
  "note2=The Second Note Second",
  "note3=The Third Note Third",
  "changeMe=Old Value"
]
→ dqs-samples git:(master) ✗
```

Environment variables can be set (or overridden) when a container is run using the --env parameter. Here, we see this feature in action:

```
→ dqs-samples git:(master) ✗ docker container run --rm --env changeMe="New Value" --env adhoc="run time"  env-demo:1.0 env
PATH=/usr/local/sbin:/usr/local/bin:/usr/sbin:/usr/bin:/sbin:/bin
HOSTNAME=e4cf4eff138f
changeMe=New Value
adhoc=run time
appDescription=This app is a sample of using ENV instructions
appName=env-demo
note1=The First Note First
note2=The Second Note Second
note3=The Third Note Third
HOME=/root
→ dqs-samples git:(master) ✗
```

It is important to know that using ENV instructions create a zero-byte-sized additional layer in the resulting image. If you are adding more than one environment variable to your image and can use the form of the instruction that supports setting multiple variables with one instruction, doing so will only create a single additional image layer, so that is the way to go.

The ARG instruction

Sometimes when building Docker images, you may need to use variable data to customize the build. The ARG instruction is the tool to handle that situation. To use it, you add ARG instructions to your Dockerfile, and then when you execute the build command, you pass in the variable data with a --build-arg parameter. The --build-arg parameter uses the now familiar key-value pair format:

```
# The ARG instruction syntax
ARG <varname>[=<default value>]

# The build-arg parameter syntax
docker image build --build-arg <varname>[=<value>] ...
```

You can use multiple ARG instructions in your Dockerfile with corresponding --build-arg parameters on the docker image build commands. You have to include an ARG instruction for every use of the --build-arg parameter. Without the ARG instruction, the --build-arg parameter will not be set during the build, and you will get a warning message. If you do not provide a --build-arg parameter or you do not provide the value part of the key-value pair for a --build-arg parameter for an existing ARG instruction, and that ARG instruction includes a default value, then the variable will be assigned the default value.

Be aware that during the image build, even though `--build-arg` is included as a parameter of the docker image build command, the corresponding variable does not get set until the ARG instruction is reached in the Dockerfile. Said another way, the value of the key-value pair of a `--build-arg` parameter will never be set until after its corresponding ARG line in the Dockerfile.

The parameters defined in ARG instructions do not persist into containers run from the created image, however, ARG instructions create new zero-byte-sized layers in the resulting images. Here is an educational example of using the ARG instruction:

```
# ARG instruction Dockerfile for Docker Quick Start
FROM alpine
LABEL maintainer="Earl Waud <earlwaud@mycompany.com>"

ENV key1="ENV is stronger than an ARG"
RUN echo ${key1}
ARG key1="not going to matter"
RUN echo ${key1}

RUN echo ${key2}
ARG key2="defaultValue"
RUN echo ${key2}
ENV key2="ENV value takes over"
RUN echo ${key2}
CMD ["sh"]
```

Create a Dockerfile with the contents shown in the preceding code block and run the following build command to see how the scope of the ENV and ARG instructions play out:

```
# Build the image and look at the output from the echo commands
docker image build --rm \
--build-arg key1="buildTimeValue" \
--build-arg key2="good till env instruction" \
--tag arg-demo:2.0 .
```

You will see by the first `echo ${key1}` that even though there is a `--build-arg` parameter for `key1`, it will not be stored as `key1` because there is an ENV instruction that has the same key name. This still holds true for the second `echo ${key1}`, which is after the ARG `key1` instruction. The ENV variable values will always be the winner when there are both ARG and EVN instructions with the same key name.

Then, you will see that the first `echo ${key2}` is empty even though there is a `--build-arg` parameter for it. It is empty because we have not reached the `ARG key2` instruction yet. The second `echo ${key2}` will contain the value from the corresponding `--build-arg` parameter even though there is a default value provided in the `ARG key2` instruction. The final `echo ${key2}` will show the value provided in the `ENV key2` instruction in spite of there being both a default value in the `ARG` and a value passed in via the `--build-arg` parameter. Again, this is because `ENV` always trumps ARG.

The difference between ENV and ARG

Again, here is a pair of instructions that have a similar functionality. They both can be used during the build of an image, setting parameters to be available to use within other Dockerfile instructions. The other Dockerfile instructions that can use these parameters are `FROM, LABEL, COPY, ADD, ENV, USER, WORKDIR, RUN, VOLUME, EXPOSE, STOPSIGNAL,` and `ONBUILD`. Here is an example of using the `ARG` and `ENV` variables in other Docker commands:

```
# ENV vs ARG instruction Dockerfile for Docker Quick Start
FROM alpine
LABEL maintainer="Earl Waud <earlwaud@mycompany.com>"
ENV lifecycle="production"
RUN echo ${lifecycle}
ARG username="35"
RUN echo ${username}
ARG appdir
RUN echo ${appdir}
ADD hello /${appdir}/
RUN chown -R ${username}:${username} ${appdir}
WORKDIR ${appdir}
USER ${username}
CMD ["./hello"]
```

With this Dockerfile, you would want to provide `--build-arg` parameters for the `appdir` ARG instruction, and the username (if you want to override the default) to the build command. You could also provide an `--env` parameter at runtime to override the lifecycle variable. Here are possible build and run commands you could use:

```
# Build the arg3 demo image
docker image build --rm \
   --build-arg appdir="/opt/hello" \
   --tag arg-demo:3.0 .

# Run the arg3 demo container
docker container run --rm --env lifecycle="test" arg-demo:3.0
```

While the ENV and ARG instructions might seem similar, they are actually quite different. Here are the key differences to remember between the parameters created by the ENV and ARG instructions:

- ENVs persist into running containers, ARGs do not.
- ARGs use corresponding build parameters, ENVs do not.
- ENV instructions must include both a key and a value, ARG instructions have a key but the (default) value is optional.
- ENVs are more significant than ARGs.

 You should never use either ENV or ARG instructions to provide secret data to the build command or resulting containers because the values are always visible in clear text to any user that runs the docker history command.

The USER instruction

The USER instruction allows you to set the current user (and group) for all of the instructions that follow in the Dockerfile, and for the containers that are run from the built image. The syntax for the USER instruction is as follows:

```
# User instruction syntax
USER <user>[:<group>] or
USER <UID>[:<GID>]
```

If a named user (or group) is provided as parameters to the USER instruction, that user (and group) must already exist in the passwd file (or group file) of the system, or a build error will occur. If you provide the UID (or GID) as the parameter to the USER command, the check to see whether the user (or group) exists is not performed. Consider the following Dockerfile:

```
# USER instruction Dockerfile for Docker Quick Start
FROM alpine
LABEL maintainer="Earl Waud <earl@mycompany.com>"
RUN id
USER games:games
run id
CMD ["sh"]
```

When the image build starts, the current user is root or UID=0 GID=0. Then, the USER instruction is executed to set the current user and group to games:games. Since this is the last use of the USER instruction in the Dockerfile, all containers run using the built image will have the current user (and group) set to games. Here is what the build and run look like:

```
→ user-demo git:(master) ✗ docker image build --rm --tag user-demo:1.0 .
Sending build context to Docker daemon  2.048kB
Step 1/6 : FROM alpine
 ---> 11cd0b38bc3c
Step 2/6 : LABEL maintainer="Earl Waud <earl@mycompany.com>"
 ---> Running in 0fc2348732c4
Removing intermediate container 0fc2348732c4
 ---> f799542505a4
Step 3/6 : RUN id
 ---> Running in b3fe2b1a9594
uid=0(root) gid=0(root) groups=0(root),1(bin),2(daemon),3(sys),4(adm),6(disk),10(wheel),11(floppy),20(dialout),26(tape),27(video)
Removing intermediate container b3fe2b1a9594
 ---> 9ef9b3864413
Step 4/6 : USER games:games
 ---> Running in 8c53373b9374
Removing intermediate container 8c53373b9374
 ---> 70a9b641ac50
Step 5/6 : run id
 ---> Running in 77c1d4f0ce3d
uid=35(games) gid=35(games)
Removing intermediate container 77c1d4f0ce3d
 ---> 3667631e8d45
Step 6/6 : CMD ["sh"]
 ---> Running in 1b3c010dacab
Removing intermediate container 1b3c010dacab
 ---> bde6fa1eb88e
Successfully built bde6fa1eb88e
Successfully tagged user-demo:1.0
→ user-demo git:(master) ✗ docker container run --rm user-demo:1.0 id
uid=35(games) gid=35(games)
→ user-demo git:(master) ✗ ▊
```

Notice that the output from **Step 3/6:RUN id** shows the current user as root, and then in **Step 5/6** (which is after the USER instruction) it shows the current user as games. Finally, notice that the container run from the image has the current user games. The USER instruction creates a zero-byte-sized layer in the image.

The WORKDIR instruction

We have seen the WORKDIR instruction used in some of the examples used to demonstrate other instructions. It is sort of like a combination of the Linux cd and mkdir commands. The WORKDIR instruction will change the current working directory in the image to the value provided in the instruction. If any segment of the path in the parameter of the WORKDIR instruction does not yet exist, it will be created as part of the execution of the instruction. The syntax for the WORKDIR instruction is as follows:

```
# WORKDIR instruction syntax
WORKDIR instruction syntax
WORKDIR /path/to/workdir
```

The WORKDIR instruction can use ENV or ARG parameter values for all or part of its parameter. A Dockerfile can have more than one WORKDIR instruction, and each subsequent WORKDIR instruction will be relative to the previous one (if a relative path is used). Here is an example that demonstrates this possibility:

```
# WORKDIR instruction Dockerfile for Docker Quick Start
FROM alpine
# Absolute path...
WORKDIR /
# relative path, relative to previous WORKDIR instruction
# creates new folder
WORKDIR sub-folder-level-1
RUN touch file1.txt
# relative path, relative to previous WORKDIR instruction
# creates new folder
WORKDIR sub-folder-level-2
RUN touch file2.txt
# relative path, relative to previous WORKDIR instruction
# creates new folder
WORKDIR sub-folder-level-3
RUN touch file3.txt
# Absolute path, creates three sub folders...
WORKDIR /11/12/13
CMD ["sh"]
```

Building the image from this Dockerfile will result in the image having three levels of nested folders. Running a container from the image and listing the files and folders will look like this:

```
→ dqs-samples git:(master) ✗ docker container run --rm workdir-demo:1.0 ls -lR /sub-folder-level-1
/sub-folder-level-1:
total 4
-rw-r--r--   1 root     root        0 Aug  6 05:11 file1.txt
drwxr-xr-x   1 root     root     4096 Aug  6 05:11 sub-folder-level-2

/sub-folder-level-1/sub-folder-level-2:
total 4
-rw-r--r--   1 root     root        0 Aug  6 05:11 file2.txt
drwxr-xr-x   1 root     root     4096 Aug  6 05:11 sub-folder-level-3

/sub-folder-level-1/sub-folder-level-2/sub-folder-level-3:
total 0
-rw-r--r--   1 root     root        0 Aug  6 05:11 file3.txt
→ dqs-samples git:(master) ✗ █
```

The WORKDIR instruction will create a zero-byte-sized layer in the resulting image.

The VOLUME instruction

You should remember that a Docker image is made up of a series of read-only layers built upon one another, and that when you run a container from a Docker image, it creates a new read-write layer that you can think of as being on top of the read-only layers. All the changes to the container are applied to the read-write layer. If you make a change to a file found in one of the read-only layers, a copy of that file is made and added to the read-write layer. Then, all the changes are applied to the copy. The copy hides the version found in the read-only layer so, from the point of view of the running container, there is only one version of the file, and it is the one that has been changed. This is roughly how the Unified File System works.

This is actually a great thing. However, it presents a challenge, this being that when the running container exits and is removed, all of the changes are removed with it. This is normally OK until you want to have some data that persists after the life of the container, or when you want to share data between containers. Docker has an instruction to help you solve this issue, the VOLUME instruction.

The VOLUME instruction will create a storage location that is outside of the United File System, and by so doing, allow storage to persist beyond the life of your container. Here is the syntax of the VOLUME instruction:

```
# VOLUME instruction syntax
VOLUME ["/data"]
# or for creating multiple volumes with a single instruction
VOLUME /var/log /var/db /moreData
```

Other ways to create volumes are to add volume parameters to the docker container run command or to use the docker volume create command. We will cover those methods in detail in Chapter 4, *Docker Volumes*.

Here is a simple example Dockerfile. It creates a volume at /myvol that will have a file named greeting:

```
# VOLUME instruction Dockerfile for Docker Quick Start
FROM alpine
RUN mkdir /myvol
RUN echo "hello world" > /myvol/greeting
VOLUME /myvol
CMD ["sh"]
```

Running a container based on an image made from this Dockerfile will create a mount point on the host system that initially contains the greeting file. When the container exits, the mount point will remain. Be careful with the use of the --rm parameter when running a container that has mount points you wish to persist. Using --rm, with no other volume parameters, will cause the mount points to be cleaned up along with the container when it exits. Here is what that looks like:

```
earl@ubuntu:~/repos/dqs-samples/volume-demo$ docker volume ls
DRIVER              VOLUME NAME
earl@ubuntu:~/repos/dqs-samples/volume-demo$ docker container run --rm -d --name vol-demo volume-demo:1.0 tail -f /dev/null
059ef9c0c17cd8a831ae27518c176a69d8453aea121eb236382bcf562361dd71
earl@ubuntu:~/repos/dqs-samples/volume-demo$ docker volume ls
DRIVER              VOLUME NAME
local               75b8fd8fd382d93c7da67403898646ca532c0ab218b41fb380ca00be8702cbc4
earl@ubuntu:~/repos/dqs-samples/volume-demo$ docker container stop vol-demo
vol-demo
earl@ubuntu:~/repos/dqs-samples/volume-demo$ docker volume ls
DRIVER              VOLUME NAME
earl@ubuntu:~/repos/dqs-samples/volume-demo$ 
```

We start out with no volumes. Then, we run a container based on the image made from the preceding Dockerfile in detached mode. We check the volumes again, and we see the volume created by running the container. Then, we stop the container and check for volumes again, and the volume is now gone. Usually, the purpose of using a VOLUME instruction is to have data in a mount point that persists after the container is gone. So, if you are going to use --rm when you run a container, you should include the --mount run parameter, which we will cover in detail in Chapter 4, *Docker Volumes*.

You can interact with the data on the host using the mount point for a volume. Here is an example that demonstrates this:

```
earl@ubuntu:~/repos$ docker container run --rm -d --name vol-demo \
>    --mount source=myvolsrc,target=/myvol \
>    volume-demo:1.0 tail -f /dev/null
cebd54aa40b0f621101fc726a54be40bd2647ebe038a6f34fe1360005cf69c9e
earl@ubuntu:~/repos$ docker volume ls
DRIVER              VOLUME NAME
local               myvolsrc
earl@ubuntu:~/repos$ docker volume inspect myvolsrc -f "{{json .Mountpoint}}"
"/var/lib/docker/volumes/myvolsrc/_data"
earl@ubuntu:~/repos$ docker container exec vol-demo ls -l /myvol
total 4
-rw-r--r--    1 root     root            12 Aug  9 03:42 greeting
earl@ubuntu:~/repos$ sudo touch /var/lib/docker/volumes/myvolsrc/_data/new-file.txt
earl@ubuntu:~/repos$ docker container exec vol-demo ls -l /myvol
total 4
-rw-r--r--    1 root     root            12 Aug  9 03:42 greeting
-rw-r--r--    1 root     root             0 Aug  9 04:24 new-file.txt
earl@ubuntu:~/repos$ 
```

In this demo, we run a container that is based on an image created with the preceding Dockerfile. Then, we list the volumes and see the **myvolsrc** volume (we already knew the name since we provided it in the run command, but you can use the ls command to find volume names that you might not otherwise know). Using the volume's name, we inspect the volume to find its mount point on the host. To verify the contents of the volume in the container, we use an exec command to do an ls of the folder. Next, using the mount point path, we create a new file using the touch command. Finally, we use the same exec command and see that inside the container the volume has been changed (from actions outside of the container). Similarly, if the container makes changes to the contents of the volume, they are reflected instantly on the host mount point.

> The preceding example will not work on OS X directly as shown. It requires some extra work. Don't panic though! We'll show you how to deal with the extra work required for OS X in Chapter 4, *Docker Volumes*.

Using the VOLUME instruction is both powerful and dangerous. It is powerful in that it lets you have data that will persist beyond the life of your containers. It is dangerous because data is passed instantaneously from the container to the host, and if the container is ever compromised, that can spell trouble. That is why, for security purposes, it is best practice to *not* include host-based VOLUME mounts in your Dockerfiles. We will cover some safer alternatives in Chapter 4, *Docker Volumes*.

The VOLUME instruction will add a zero-bytes sized layer to your resulting Docker image.

The EXPOSE instruction

The EXPOSE instruction is a way to document what network ports the image expects to be opened when a container is run from the image built using the Dockerfile. The syntax for the EXPOSE instruction is as follows:

```
# EXPOSE instruction syntax
EXPOSE <port> [<port>/<protocol>...]
```

It is important to understand that including the EXPOSE instruction in the Dockerfile does not actually open network ports in containers. When containers are run from the images with the EXPOSE instruction in their Dockerfile, it is still necessary to include the -p or -P parameters to actually open the network ports to the container.

You can include multiple EXPOSE instructions in your Dockerfile as needed. Including the -P parameter at runtime is a shortcut way to automatically open ports for all of the EXPOSE instructions included in the Dockerfile. The corresponding host ports will be randomly assigned when using the -P parameter on the run command.

Think of the EXPOSE instruction as a message from the image developer telling you that the application in the image is expecting you to open the indicated port(s) when you run your containers. The EXPOSE instruction creates a zero-byte-sized layer in the resulting image.

The RUN instruction

The RUN instruction is the real workhorse of the Dockerfile. It is the tool by which you affect the most change in the resulting docker image. Basically, it allows you to execute any command in the image. There are two forms of the RUN instruction. Here is the syntax:

```
# RUN instruction syntax
# Shell form to run the command in a shell
```

```
# For Linux the default is "/bin/sh -c"
# For Windows the default is "cmd /S /C"
RUN <command>


# Exec form
RUN ["executable", "param1", "param2"]
```

Every RUN instruction creates a new layer in the image, and the layers for each instruction that follow will be built on the results of the RUN instruction's layer. The shell form of the instruction will use the default shell unless it is overridden using a SHELL instruction, which we will discuss in *The SHELL instruction* section. If you are building a container that does not include a shell, you will need to use the exec form of the RUN instruction. You can also use the exec form of the instruction to use a different shell. For example, to run a command using the bash shell, you could add a RUN instruction, like so:

```
# Exec form of RUN instruction using bash
RUN ["/bin/bash", "-c", "echo hello world > /myvol/greeting"]
```

The uses for the RUN command are limited only by the imagination, so providing an exhaustive list of RUN instruction samples would be impossible, but here are a few using both forms of the instruction, just to give you some ideas:

```
# RUN instruction Dockerfile for Docker Quick Start
FROM ubuntu
RUN useradd --create-home -m -s /bin/bash dev
RUN mkdir /myvol
RUN echo "hello DQS Guide" > /myvol/greeting
RUN ["chmod", "664", "/myvol/greeting"]
RUN ["chown", "dev:dev", "/myvol/greeting"]
VOLUME /myvol
USER dev
CMD ["/bin/bash"]
```

There is a fun and useful RUN instruction you can add when you know your image will include bash. This idea was shared with me by my colleague *Marcello de Sales* after he learned of it at Dockercon 16.

You can use the following code to create a custom prompt displayed when you shell into your containers. If you don't like the whale graphic, you can switch it up and use anything you like better. I've included some of my favorite options. Here's the code:

```
# RUN instruction Dockerfile for Docker Quick Start
FROM ubuntu
RUN useradd --create-home -m -s /bin/bash dev
# Add a fun prompt for dev user of my-app
# whale: "\xF0\x9F\x90\xB3"
```

```
# alien:"\xF0\x9F\x91\xBD"
# fish:"\xF0\x9F\x90\xA0"
# elephant:"\xF0\x9F\x91\xBD"
# moneybag:"\xF0\x9F\x92\xB0"
RUN echo 'PS1="\[$(tput bold)$(tput setaf 4)\]my-app $(echo -e
"\xF0\x9F\x90\xB3") \[$(tput sgr0)\] [\\u@\\h]:\\W \\$ "' >>
/home/dev/.bashrc && \
    echo 'alias ls="ls --color=auto"' >> /home/dev/.bashrc
USER dev
CMD ["/bin/bash"]
```

The resulting prompt looks like this:

```
→ dqs-samples git:(master) ✗ docker container run --rm -it run-demo:1.0
my-app 🐳 [dev@374f0fdf7914]:/ $ ▊
```

The CMD instruction

The CMD instruction is used to define the default action taken when containers are run from images built with their Dockerfile. While it is possible to include more than one CMD instruction in a Dockerfile, only the last one will be significant. Essentially, the final CMD instruction provides the default action for the image. This allows you to either override or use the CMD in the image used in the FROM instruction of your Dockerfile. Here is an example where a trivial Dockerfile does not contain a CMD instruction and relies on the one found in the ubuntu image used in the FROM instruction:

```
→ dqs-samples git:(master) ✗ docker history ubuntu
IMAGE              CREATED          CREATED BY                                    SIZE
735f80812f90       2 weeks ago      /bin/sh -c #(nop)  CMD ["/bin/bash"]          0B
<missing>          2 weeks ago      /bin/sh -c mkdir -p /run/systemd && echo 'do… 7B
<missing>          2 weeks ago      /bin/sh -c sed -i 's/^#\s*\(deb.*universe\)$… 2.76kB
<missing>          2 weeks ago      /bin/sh -c rm -rf /var/lib/apt/lists/*        0B
<missing>          2 weeks ago      /bin/sh -c set -xe    && echo '#!/bin/sh' > /… 745B
<missing>          2 weeks ago      /bin/sh -c #(nop) ADD file:4bb62bb0587406855… 83.5MB
→ dqs-samples git:(master) ✗ cat cmd-demo/Dockerfile
# CMD instruction Dockerfile for Docker Quick Start
FROM ubuntu
→ dqs-samples git:(master) ✗ docker container run --rm -it cmd-demo:1.0
root@4f752d8d4254:/# exit
exit
→ dqs-samples git:(master) ✗ ▊
```

You can see from the output of the history command that the ubuntu image includes the CMD ["/bin/bash"] instruction. You will also see that our Dockerfile does not have its own CMD instruction. When we run the container, the default action is to run "/bin/bash".

There are three forms of the CMD instruction. The first is a shell form. The second is an exec form, which is the best practice form to use. And, the third is a special exec form that has exactly two parameters, and it is used in conjunction with the ENTRYPOINT instruction, which we will talk about in *The ENTRYPOINT instruction* section. Here is the syntax for the CMD instruction.

```
# CMD instruction syntax
CMD command param1 param2 (shell form)
CMD ["executable","param1","param2"] (exec form)
CMD ["param1","param2"] (as default parameters to ENTRYPOINT)
```

Here are a few CMD instruction examples for your enjoyment:

```
# CMD instruction examples
CMD ["/bin/bash"]
CMD while true; do echo 'DQS Expose Demo' | nc -l -p 80; done
CMD echo "How many words are in this echo command" | wc -
CMD tail -f /dev/null
CMD ["-latr", "/var/opt"]
```

Like the RUN instruction, the shell form of the CMD instruction will use the ["/bin/sh", "-c"] shell command (or ["cmd", "/S", "/C"] for Windows) by default unless it is overridden with a SHELL instruction. However, unlike the RUN instruction, the CMD instruction does not execute anything during the building of the image but instead is executed when containers built from the image are run. If the container image being built will not have a shell, then the exec form of the instruction can be used as it does not invoke a shell. The CMD instruction adds a zero-byte-sized layer to the image.

The ENTRYPOINT instruction

The ENTRYPOINT instruction is used to configure a docker image to run like an application or a command. For example, we can use the ENTRYPOINT instruction to make an image that displays help for the curl command. Consider this Dockerfile:

```
# ENTRYPOINT instruction Dockerfile for Docker Quick Start
FROM alpine
RUN apk add curl
ENTRYPOINT ["curl"]
CMD ["--help"]
```

We can run the container image with no overriding CMD parameter and it will show help for the curl command. However, when we run the container with a CMD override parameter, in this case, a URL, the response will be to curl the URL. Take a look:

```
→  dqs-samples git:(master) ✗ docker container run entrypoint-demo:1.0 google.com
  % Total    % Received % Xferd  Average Speed   Time    Time     Time  Current
                                 Dload  Upload   Total   Spent    Left  Speed
100   219  100   219    0     0   3910      0 --:--:-- --:--:-- --:--:--  3910
<HTML><HEAD><meta http-equiv="content-type" content="text/html;charset=utf-8">
<TITLE>301 Moved</TITLE></HEAD><BODY>
<H1>301 Moved</H1>
The document has moved
<A HREF="http://www.google.com/">here</A>.
</BODY></HTML>
```

When run parameters are provided to a container that has the exec form of the ENTRYPOINT command, those parameters will be appended to the ENTRYPOINT instruction, overriding anything provided in a CMD instruction. In this example, --help is overridden with the google.com run parameter, so the resulting instruction is curl google.com. Here is the actual syntax for the ENTRYPOINT instruction:

```
# ENTRYPOINT instruction syntax
ENTRYPOINT command param1 param2 (shell form)
ENTRYPOINT ["executable", "param1", "param2"] (exec form, best practice)
```

Like the CMD instruction, only the last ENTRYPOINT instruction is significant. Again, this allows you to either use or override the ENTRYPOINT instruction in the FROM image used. Like both the RUN and CMD instructions, using the shell form will invoke a shell as ["/bin/sh", "-c"] (or ["cmd", "/S", "/C"] on Windows). This is not the case when using the exec form of the instruction. This is key if you have an image that does not have a shell or if the shell is not available to the active user context. However, you will not get shell processing, so any shell environment variables will not get substituted when using the exec form of the instruction. It is generally considered best practice to use the exec form of the ENTRYPOINT instruction whenever possible.

The difference between CMD and ENTRYPOINT

Here again, we have two instructions that on the surface seem to be very much the same. It is true that there is some overlap of functionality between the two. Both instructions provide a way to define a default application that is executed when containers are run. However, they each serve their own unique purpose, and in some cases work together to provide greater functionality than either instruction alone.

The best practice is to use the ENTRYPOINT instruction when you want a container to execute as an application, providing a specific (developer) defined function, and to use CMD when you want to give the user more flexibility in what function the container will serve.

Both of these instructions have two forms: a shell form and an exec form. It is best practice to use the exec form of either whenever possible. The reason for this is that the shell form, by definition, will run `["/bin/sh", "-c"]` (or `["cmd", "/S", "/C"]` on Windows) to launch the application in the parameter of the instruction. Because of this, the primary process running in the container is not the application. Instead, it is the shell. This affects how the container exits, it affects how signals are processed, and it can really cause problems for images that do not include `"/bin/sh"`. One use case where you might need to use the shell form is if you require shell-environment-variable substitution.

There is also a use case for using both instructions in your Dockerfile. When you use both, you can define a specific application that gets executed when the container is run, and allow the user to easily provide the parameters that get used with the defined application. In this scenario, you would use the ENTRYPOINT instruction to set the application being executed and provide a default set of parameters for the application using the CMD instruction. With this configuration, the user of the container can benefit from the default parameters supplied in the CMD instruction, or they can easily override those parameters used in the application by supplying them as arguments in the `container run` command. It is highly recommended that you use the exec form of both instructions when you use them together.

The HEALTHCHECK instruction

The HEALTHCHECK instruction, which is a fairly new addition to the Dockerfile, is used to define the command to run inside a container to test the container's application health. When a container has a HEALTHCHECK, it gets a special status variable. Initially, that variable will be set to starting. Any time a HEALTHCHECK is performed successfully, the status will be set to healthy. When a HEALTHCHECK is performed and fails, the fail count value will be incremented and then checked against a retries value. If the fail count equals or exceeds the retries value, the status is set to unhealthy. The syntax of the HEALTHCHECK instruction is as follows:

```
# HEALTHCHECK instruction syntax
HEALTHCHECK [OPTIONS] CMD command (check container health by running a
command inside the container)
HEALTHCHECK NONE (disable any HEALTHCHECK inherited from the base image)
```

There are four options that can be used when setting the HEALTHCHECK, and these options are as follows:

```
# HEALTHCHECK CMD options
--interval=DURATION (default: 30s)
--timeout=DURATION (default: 30s)
--start-period=DURATION (default: 0s)
--retries=N (default: 3)
```

The --interval option allows you to define the amount of time between the HEALTHCHECK tests. The --timeout option allows you to define the amount of time that is considered too long for a HEALTHCHECK test. If the timeout is exceeded, the test is automatically considered a failure. The --start-period option allows for the definition of a no-fail time period during the container startup. Finally, the --retries option allows you to define how many consecutive failures it takes to update the HEALTHCHECK status to unhealthy.

The CMD part of the HEALTHCHECK instruction follows the same rules as the CMD instruction. Please review the preceding section regarding the CMD instruction for complete details. The CMD that is used will provide a status when it exits, which will be either a 0 for success or a 1 for fail. Here is a Dockerfile example that uses the HEALTHCHECK instruction:

```
# HEALTHCHECK instruction Dockerfile for Docker Quick Start
FROM alpine
RUN apk add curl
EXPOSE 80/tcp
HEALTHCHECK --interval=30s --timeout=3s \
  CMD curl -f http://localhost/ || exit 1
CMD while true; do echo 'DQS Expose Demo' | nc -l -p 80; done
```

Running a container from an image built with the preceding Dockerfile looks like this:

```
→ dqs-samples git:(master) ✗ docker container run --rm -d -p 80:80 --name health healthcheck-demo:1.0
5602c16ec8f5d6f1a52c6bc628796c8c308a16f25fdef4eaee6bc80a09009920
→ dqs-samples git:(master) ✗ docker container ls
CONTAINER ID   IMAGE                COMMAND            CREATED         STATUS                        PORTS                  NAMES
5602c16ec8f5   healthcheck-demo:1.0 "/bin/sh -c 'while t..." 5 seconds ago  Up 3 seconds (health: starting)  0.0.0.0:80->80/tcp   health
→ dqs-samples git:(master) ✗ docker container ls
CONTAINER ID   IMAGE                COMMAND            CREATED         STATUS                        PORTS                  NAMES
5602c16ec8f5   healthcheck-demo:1.0 "/bin/sh -c 'while t..." About a minute ago Up About a minute (healthy)  0.0.0.0:80->80/tcp   health
→ dqs-samples git:(master) ✗
```

You can see that the HEALTHCHECK initially reported a status of starting, but once the HEALTHCHECK CMD reported success, the status updated to healthy.

The ONBUILD instruction

The ONBUILD instruction is a tool used when creating images that will become the parameter to the FROM instructions in another Dockerfile. The ONBUILD instruction just adds metadata to your image, specifically a trigger that is stored in the image and not otherwise used. However, that metadata trigger does get used when your image is supplied as the parameter in the FROM command of another Dockerfile. Here is the ONBUILD instruction syntax:

```
# ONBUILD instruction syntax
ONBUILD [INSTRUCTION]
```

The ONBUILD instruction is kind of like a Docker time machine used to send instructions into the future. (You might laugh if you knew how many times I just typed *Doctor time machine!*) Let's demonstrate the use of the ONBUILD instruction with a simple example. First, we will build an image named my-base using the following Dockerfile:

```
# my-base Dockerfile
FROM alpine
LABEL maintainer="Earl Waud <earlwaud@mycompany.com>"
ONBUILD LABEL version="1.0"
ONBUILD LABEL support-email="support@mycompany.com" support-phone="(123)
456-7890"
CMD ["sh"]
```

Next, let's build an image named my-app that is built FROM the my-base image, like so:

```
# my-app Dockerfile
FROM my-base:1.0
CMD ["sh"]
```

Inspecting the resulting my-app image shows us that the LABEL commands provided in the ONBUILD instructions were sent forward in time, arriving at the my-app image:

```
→ dqs-samples git:(master) ✗ docker image inspect --format "{{json .Config}}" my-app:1.0 | jq '.Labels'
{
  "maintainer": "Earl Waud <earlwaud@mycompany.com>",
  "support-email": "support@mycompany.com",
  "support-phone": "(123) 456-7890",
  "version": "1.0"
}
→ dqs-samples git:(master) ✗ █
```

If you did a similar inspect of the my-base image, you would find that it does *not* contain the version and support labels. Note also that the ONBUILD instruction is a one-time-use time machine. If you were to build a new image using the my-app in the FROM instruction, the new image would *not* get the labels that were provided in the ONBUILD instructions of the my-base image.

The STOPSIGNAL instruction

The STOPSIGNAL instruction is used to set the system call signal that will be sent to the container to tell it to exit. The parameter used in the instruction can be an unsigned number, which equals a position in the kernel's syscall table, or it can be an actual signal name in uppercase. Here is the syntax for the instruction:

```
# STOPSIGNAL instruction syntax
STOPSIGNAL signal
```

Examples of the STOPSIGNAL instruction include the following:

```
# Sample STOPSIGNAL instruction using a position number in the syscall
table
STOPSIGNAL 9
# or using a signal name
STOPSIGNAL SIGQUIT
```

The parameter supplied to the STOPSIGNAL instruction is used when a docker container stop command is issued. Remember that it is vital to use the exec form of your ENTRYPOINT and/or CMD instructions so that the application is PID 1, and will receive the signals directly. Here is a link to an excellent blog post on using signals with Docker: https://medium.com/@gchudnov/trapping-signals-in-docker-containers-7a57fdda7d86. The article provides an excellent example of using a node.js app to handle the signals, complete with code and Dockerfile.

The SHELL instruction

As you have read in many sections throughout this chapter, there are several instructions that take two forms, the exec form or the shell form. As mentioned, the default used by all of the shell forms is ["/bin/sh", "-c"] for Linux containers, and ["cmd", "/S", "/C"] for Windows containers. The SHELL instruction allows you to change that default. Here is the syntax for the SHELL instruction:

```
# SHELL instruction syntax
SHELL ["executable", "parameters"]
```

The SHELL instruction can be used more than once in a Dockerfile. All instructions that use a shell, and that come after a SHELL instruction, will use the new shell. Thus, you can change the shell multiple times in a single Dockerfile as needed. This can be especially powerful when creating Windows containers since it allows you to switch back and forth between using cmd.exe and powershell.exe.

The Docker image build command

OK, so the image build command is not a Dockerfile instruction. Instead, it is the docker command that is used to turn your Dockerfile into a docker image. The Docker image build command sends the docker build context, including the Dockerfile, to the docker daemon, which parses the Dockerfile and builds the image layer by layer. We will discuss the build context shortly, but for now, consider it to be everything that is needed to build the Docker image based on the content found in the Dockerfile. The build command syntax is as follows:

```
# Docker image build command syntax
Usage: docker image build [OPTIONS] PATH | URL | -
```

There are many options for the image build command. We will not be covering all of the options now, but let's take a look at a few of the most common:

```
# Common options used with the image build command
--rm          Remove intermediate containers after a successful build
--build-arg   Set build-time variables
--tag         Name and optionally a tag in the 'name:tag' format
--file        Name of the Dockerfile (Default is 'PATH/Dockerfile')
```

The Docker daemon builds the image by creating a new image from each command in the Dockerfile. Each new image is built upon the previous. Using the optional `--rm` parameter will instruct the daemon to delete all the intermediate images when the build completes successfully. Using this will slow the build process when you rebuild a successfully built image, but will keep the local image cache cleaner.

We have already talked about build args when we covered the ARG instruction. Remember that the `--build-arg` option is how you provide a value to the ARG instruction in the Dockerfile.

The `--tag` option allows you to give your images a more human-readable name and version. We have seen this option used in several of the earlier examples as well.

The `--file` option allows you to use a filename other than Dockerfile, and to keep the Dockerfile in a path other than the build context folder.

Here are some image build commands for reference:

```
# build command samples
docker image build --rm --build-arg username=35 --tag arg-demo:2.0 .
docker image build --rm --tag user-demo:1.0 .
docker image build --rm --tag workdir-demo:1.0 .
```

You will notice the trailing . in each of the preceding examples. This period is indicating that the current working directory is the root of the build context for the image build.

Parser Directives

Parser Directives are a special subset of optional comment lines in the Dockerfile. Any parser directives must occur before the first normal comment line. They must also precede any blank lines or other build instructions, including the FROM instruction. Basically, all parser directives must be at the very top of the Dockerfile. By the way, if you haven't figured it out yet, you can create a normal comment line in a Dockerfile by starting that line with a # character. The syntax for a parser directive is as follows:

```
# directive=value
# The line above shows the syntax for a parser directive
```

So, what can you do with a parser directive? Well right now, the only one supported is escape. The escape parser directive is used to change what character is used to indicate that the next character in the instruction is to be treated as a character and not as the special character it represents. The default value if no parser directive is used is \. You have seen this used in several examples throughout this chapter to escape the newline character, allowing for instructions to be continued onto the next line in the Dockerfile. If it is necessary to use a different escape character, you can use the escape parser directive to handle that. You can set the escape character to one of two choices:

```
# escape=\ (backslash)
Or
# escape=` (backtick)
```

One example where you might want to change the character used as the escape character is when you are creating a Dockerfile on Windows systems. As you know, the \ is used to distinguish folder levels in path strings, such as c:\windows\system32 \drivers. Switching to the backtick for the escape character will avoid needing to escape such strings as this: c:\\windows\\system32\\drivers.

The build context

The build context is everything that gets sent to the Docker daemon when using the build image command. This includes the Dockerfile and the contents of the current working directory when the build command is issued, including all subdirectories that the current working directory may contain. It is possible to have the Dockerfile in a directory other than the current working directory by using a -f or --file option, but the Dockerfile still gets sent with the build context. Using the .dockerignore file, you can exclude files and folders from the build context when it gets sent to the Docker daemon.

When building Docker images, it is very important to keep the build context as small as possible. This is because the entire build context is sent to the Docker daemon for building the image. If you have unnecessary files and folders in the build context, then it will slow the build process, and depending on the contents of the Dockerfile, can result in bloated images. This is such an important consideration, that every image build command displays the size of the build context as the first line of the command's output. It looks like this:

```
→ dqs-samples git:(master) make healthcheck
cd healthcheck-demo && \
        docker image build --rm --tag healthcheck-demo:1.0 .
Sending build context to Docker daemon   2.048kB
Step 1/5 : FROM alpine
 ---> 11cd0b38bc3c
Step 2/5 : RUN apk add curl
```

The build context becomes the filesystem root for the commands in the Dockerfile. For example, consider using the following COPY instruction:

```
# build context Dockerfile for Docker Quick Start guide
FROM scratch
COPY hello /
CMD ["/hello"]
```

This tells the Docker daemon to copy the hello file from the root of the build context into the root of the container image.

If the command completes successfully, the image ID will be displayed, and if a --
tag option is provided, the new tag and version will be shown as well:

```
Step 5/5 : CMD while true; do echo 'DQS Expose Demo' | nc -l -p 80; done
 ---> Using cache
 ---> d5b65cfcd612
Successfully built d5b65cfcd612
Successfully tagged healthcheck-demo:1.0
➜ dqs-samples git:(master)
```

One of the keys to keeping the build context small is the use of a .dockerignore file.

The .dockerignore file

If you are familiar with using .gitignore files, then you will already have a basic
understanding of the purpose for the .dockerignore file. The .dockerignore file is used
to exclude files that you do not want to be included with the build context during a docker
image build. Using it helps to prevent sensitive and other unwanted files from being
included in the build context, and potentially in the docker image. It is an excellent tool to
help keep your Docker images small.

The .dockerignore file needs to be in the root folder of the build context. Like a
.gitignore file, it uses a newline-separated list of patterns. Comments in the
.dockerignore file are denoted by a # as the first character of a line. You can override a
pattern by including an exception line. An exception line is denoted with a ! as the first
character of the line. All other lines are considered patterns to use to exclude files and/or
folders.

Line order in the .dockerignore file is significant. Matching patterns of lines later in the
file will override matching lines earlier in the file. If you add a pattern that matches the
.dockerignore file or the Dockerfile file, they will still be sent to the docker daemon with
the build context, but they will not be available to any ADD or COPY instructions, and
therefore cannot end up in the resulting image. Here is an example:

```
# Example of a .dockerignore file
# Exclude unwanted files
**/*~
**/*.log
**/.DS_Store
```

Summary

OK! That was an adventure. You should now be able to build any type of Docker image that your heart desires. You know when to use COPY versus ADD, when to use ENV versus ARG, and perhaps most importantly, when to use CMD versus ENTERYPOINT. You even learned how to travel through time! This information is really a great foundation for getting started with Docker and will serve as a great reference as you develop more complex Docker images.

I hope you have learned a lot from this chapter, but we still have more to learn, so let's turn our attention to the next topic. In Chapter 4, *Docker Volumes*, we are going to learn more about Docker volumes. Turn the page and let's continue our quick-start journey.

References

Check out the following links for information about topics discussed in this chapter:

- The hello-world GitHub repository: https://github.com/docker-library/hello-world
- Docker volumes: https://docs.docker.com/storage/volumes/
- Using signals with Docker: https://medium.com/@gchudnov/trapping-signals-in-docker-containers-7a57fdda7d86
- The .dockerignore reference document: https://docs.docker.com/engine/reference/builder/#dockerignore-file
- Best practices for the Dockerfile: https://docs.docker.com/v17.09/engine/userguide/eng-image/dockerfile_best-practices/

4
Docker Volumes

In this chapter, we will learn the secrets of Docker volumes. We will learn how to use folders on your workstation inside of your Docker containers, and we will learn how to create and use persistent volumes, allowing multiple containers to share data. We will learn how to clean up after unused volumes. And, to round out this chapter, we will learn how to create data-volume containers to become the source of volumes for other containers.

> *Approximately 675 shipping containers are lost at sea each year. In 1992, a 40 ft container full of toys actually fell into the Pacific Ocean and 10 months later some of its toys drifted ashore on the Alaskan coastline*
>
> —https://www.clevelandcontainers.co.uk/blog/16-fun-facts-about-containers

In this chapter, we will cover the following topics:

- What is a Docker volume?
- Creating Docker volumes
- Two ways to remove Docker volumes
- Sharing data between containers with data volume containers

Technical requirements

You will be pulling Docker images from Docker's public repo, so basic internet access is required to execute the examples within this chapter.

The code files of this chapter can be found on GitHub:
https://github.com/PacktPublishing/Docker-Quick-Start-Guide/tree/master/Chapter04

Check out the following video to see the code in action:
http://bit.ly/2QqK78a

What is a Docker volume?

As we learned in Chapter 3, *Creating Docker Images*, Docker uses a special filesystem called a **Union File System**. This is the key to Docker's layered image model and allows for many of the features that make using Docker so desirable. However, the one thing that the Union File System does not provide for is the persistent storage of data. If you recall, the layers of a Docker image are read-only. When you run a container from a Docker image, the Docker daemon creates a new read-write layer that holds all of the live data that represents your container. When your container makes changes to its filesystem, those changes go into that read-write layer. As such, when your container goes away, taking the read-write layer goes with it, and any and all changes the container made to data within that layer are deleted and gone forever. That equals non-persistent storage. Remember, however, that generally speaking this is a good thing. A great thing, in fact. Most of the time, this is exactly what we want to happen. Containers are meant to be ephemeral and their state data is too. However, there are plenty of use cases for persistent data, such as customer order data for a shopping site. It would be a pretty bad design if all the order data went bye-bye if a container crashed or had to be re-stacked.

Enter the Docker volume. The Docker volume is a storage location that is completely outside of the Union File System. As such, it is not bound by the same rules that are placed on the read-only layers of an image or the read-write layer of a container. A Docker volume is a storage location that, by default, is on the host that is running the container that uses the volume. When the container goes away, either by design or by a catastrophic event, the Docker volume stays behind and is available to use by other containers. The Docker volume can be used by more than one container at the same time.

The simplest way to describe a Docker volume is this: a Docker volume is a folder that exists on the Docker host and is mounted and accessible inside a running Docker container. The accessibility goes both ways, allowing the contents of that folder to be modified from inside the container, or on the Docker host where the folder lives.

Now, this description is a bit of a generalization. Using different volume drivers, the actual location of the folder being mounted as a volume can be hosted somewhere not on the Docker host. With volume drivers, you are able to create your volumes on remote hosts or cloud providers. For example, you can use an NFS driver to allow the creation of Docker volumes on a remote NFS server.

Like Docker image and Docker container, the volume commands represent their own management category. As you would expect, the top-level management command for volumes is as follows:

```
# Docker volume managment command
docker volume
```

The subcommands available in the volume management group include the following:

```
# Docker volume management subcommands
docker volume create          # Create a volume
docker volume inspect         # Display information on one or more volumes
docker volume ls              # List volumes
docker volume rm              # Remove one or more volumes
docker volume prune           # Remove all unused local volumes
```

There are a few different ways you can create a Docker volume, so let's continue our investigation of Docker volumes by creating some.

References

Check out the following links for more information:

- The Docker reference for using Docker volumes: `https://docs.docker.com/storage/volumes/`
- Docker volume plugin information: `https://docs.docker.com/engine/extend/plugins_volume/`
- Docker engine volume plugins: `https://docs.docker.com/engine/extend/legacy_plugins/#volume-plugins`

Creating Docker volumes

There are a few ways to create a Docker volume. One way is to use the `volume create` command. The syntax for that command is as follows:

```
# Syntax for the volume create command
Usage: docker volume create [OPTIONS] [VOLUME]
```

In addition to the optional volume name parameter, the `create` command allows for these options:

```
# The options available to the volume create command:
-d, --driver string           # Specify volume driver name (default "local")
--label list                  # Set metadata for a volume
-o, --opt map                 # Set driver specific options (default map[])
```

Let's start with the simplest example:

```
# Using the volume create command with no optional parameters
docker volume create
```

Executing the preceding command will create a new Docker volume and assign it a random name. The volume will be created using the built-in local driver (by default). Using the volume ls command, you can see what random name the Docker daemon assigned our new volume. It will look something like this:

```
earl@ubuntu:~$ docker volume create
36aad2bfbe9b8f2a193e89271149e8c2dfa8e025b5f3e32dbc86fbba7c6bac1c
earl@ubuntu:~$ docker volume ls
DRIVER              VOLUME NAME
local               36aad2bfbe9b8f2a193e89271149e8c2dfa8e025b5f3e32dbc86fbba7c6bac1c
earl@ubuntu:~$
```

Stepping it up a notch, let's create another volume, this time supplying an optional volume name with the command. The command will look something like this:

```
# Create a volume with a fancy name
docker volume create my-vol-02
```

This time, the volume is created and is given the name my-vol-02, as requested:

```
earl@ubuntu:~$ docker volume create my-vol-02
my-vol-02
earl@ubuntu:~$ docker volume ls
DRIVER              VOLUME NAME
local               36aad2bfbe9b8f2a193e89271149e8c2dfa8e025b5f3e32dbc86fbba7c6bac1c
local               my-vol-02
earl@ubuntu:~$
```

This volume still uses the default local driver. Using the local driver simply means that the actual location for the folder this volume represents can be found locally on the Docker host. We can use the volume inspect subcommand to see where that folder can actually be found:

```
earl@ubuntu: ~
earl@ubuntu:~$ docker volume inspect my-vol-02
[
    {
        "CreatedAt": "2018-08-22T23:12:16-04:00",
        "Driver": "local",
        "Labels": {},
        "Mountpoint": "/var/lib/docker/volumes/my-vol-02/_data",
        "Name": "my-vol-02",
        "Options": {},
        "Scope": "local"
    }
]
earl@ubuntu:~$ sudo ls -l /var/lib/docker/volumes/my-vol-02
total 4
drwxr-xr-x 2 root root 4096 Aug 22 23:12 _data
earl@ubuntu:~$
```

As you can see in the preceding screenshot, the volume's mount point is on the Docker host's filesystem at /var/lib/docker/volumes/my-vol-02/_data. Notice that the folder path is owned by root, which means you need elevated permissions to access the location from the host. Notice also that this example was run on a Linux host.

If you are using OS X, you need to remember that your Docker install is actually using a mostly seamless virtual machine. One of the areas where the seams do show up is with the use of the Docker volumes. The mount point that is created when you create a Docker volume on an OS X host is stored in the filesystem of the virtual machine, not on your OS X filesystem. When you use the docker volume inspect command and see the path to the mount point of your volume, it is not a path on your OS X filesystem, but rather the path on the filesystem of the hidden virtual machine.

There is a way to view the filesystem (and other features) of that hidden virtual machine. With a command, often referred to as the Magic Screen command, you can access the running Docker VM. That command looks like this:

```
# The Magic Screen command
screen ~/Library/Containers/com.docker.docker/Data
/com.docker.driver.amd64-linux/tty
# or if you are using Mac OS High Sierra
screen ~/Library/Containers/com.docker.docker/Data/vms/0/tty
```

Use *Ctrl + AK* to kill the screen session.

You can detach with *Ctrl + A Ctrl + D,* then use `screen -r` to reconnect, but don't detach and then start a new screen session. Running more than one screen to the VM will give you tty garbage.

Here is an example of accessing the mount point for a volume created on an OS X host. Here is the setup:

```
# Start by creating a new volume
docker volume create my-osx-volume
# Now find the Mountpoint
docker volume inspect my-osx-volume -f "{{json .Mountpoint}}"
# Try to view the contents of the Mountpoint's folder
sudo ls -l /var/lib/docker/volumes/my-osx-volume
# "No such file or directory" because the directory does not exist on the
OS X host
```

And here is what the setup looks like:

```
→ dqs-samples git:(master) docker volume create my-osx-volume
my-osx-volume
→ dqs-samples git:(master) docker volume inspect my-osx-volume -f "{{json .Mountpoint}}"
"/var/lib/docker/volumes/my-osx-volume/_data"
→ dqs-samples git:(master) sudo ls -l /var/lib/docker/volumes/my-osx-volume
Password:
ls: /var/lib/docker/volumes/my-osx-volume: No such file or directory
→ dqs-samples git:(master)
```

Now, here is how to use the magic screen command to accomplish what we want, which is access to the volume mountpoint:

```
# Now issue the Magic Screen command and hit <enter> to get a prompt
screen ~/Library/Containers/com.docker.docker/Data/vms/0/tty
# You are now root in the VM, and can issue the following command
ls -l /var/lib/docker/volumes/my-osx-volume
# The directory exists and you will see the actual Mountpoint sub folder
"_data"
# Now hit control-a followed by lower case k to kill the screen session
<CTRL-a>k
```

And voila...

Now is a good time to point out that we have created these volumes without ever creating or using a Docker container. This is an indication that a Docker volume is outside of the realm of the normal container-union filesystem.

We saw in `Chapter 3`, *Creating Docker Images,* that we can also create volumes using a parameter on the container run command, or by adding a `VOLUME` instruction in the Dockerfile. And, as you might expect, you are able to mount volumes pre-created using the Docker `volume create` command into containers by using a container run parameter, namely the `--mount` parameter, for example, as follows:

```
# mount a pre-created volume with --mount parameter
docker container run --rm -d \
--mount source=my-vol-02,target=/myvol \
--name vol-demo2 \
volume-demo2:1.0 tail -f /dev/null
```

This example will run a new container that will mount the existing volume named `my-vol-02`. It will mount that volume in the container at `/myvol`. Note that the preceding example could also have been run without pre-creating the `my-vol-02:volume`, and the act of running the container with the `--mount` parameter would create the volume as part of the process of starting up the container. Note that any contents defined in the image's mount point folder will be added to the volume when the volume is mounted. However, if a file exists in the image's mount point folder, it also exists in the host's mount point, and the contents of the host's file will be what ends up being in the file. Using an image from this Dockerfile, here is what that looks like:

```
# VOLUME instruction Dockerfile for Docker Quick Start
FROM alpine
RUN mkdir /myvol
RUN echo "Data from image" > /myvol/both-places.txt
CMD ["sh"]
```

Note the `Data from image` line. Now, using a pre-created volume that contains a file with the matching name of `both-places.txt`, but has the `Data from volume` contents in the file, we will run a container based on the image. Here is what happens:

```
earl@ubuntu: ~/repos/dqs-samples/chapter04
earl@ubuntu:~/repos/dqs-samples/chapter04$ docker container ls
CONTAINER ID        IMAGE              COMMAND             CREATED         STATUS          PORTS
earl@ubuntu:~/repos/dqs-samples/chapter04$ docker volume ls
DRIVER              VOLUME NAME
local               my-vol-02
earl@ubuntu:~/repos/dqs-samples/chapter04$ sudo cat /var/lib/docker/volumes/my-vol-02/_data/both-places.txt
Data from volume
earl@ubuntu:~/repos/dqs-samples/chapter04$ docker container run --rm -d \
>    --mount source=my-vol-02,target=/myvol \
>    --name vol-demo2 volume-demo2:1.0 \
>    tail -f /dev/null
d08c76fe999a3a0559cfb7e084d8363977255b7a4f85a5b2aabb1aee332630de
earl@ubuntu:~/repos/dqs-samples/chapter04$ docker container exec -it vol-demo2 /bin/sh
/ # cat /myvol/both-places.txt
Data from volume
/ # exit
earl@ubuntu:~/repos/dqs-samples/chapter04$
```

As you can see, even though the Dockerfile created a file with the `Data from image` contents, when we ran a container from that image and mounted a volume that had the same file, the contents from the volume (`Data from volume`) prevailed and is what was found in the running container.

Remember that you cannot mount a pre-created volume via a VOLUME instruction in a Dockerfile. There is no such thing as a Dockerfile VOLUME instruction named volume. The reason for this is that the Dockerfile cannot dictate the location on the host that a volume is mounted from. Allowing that would be bad for a few reasons. First, since the Dockerfile creates an image, every container that was run from that image would be trying to mount the same host location. That could get real bad real fast. Second, since a container image can be run on different host operating systems, it is quite possible that the definition of the host path for one OS would not even work on another OS. Again, bad. Third, defining the volumes host path would open up all kinds of security holes. Bad, bad, bad! Because of this, running a container from an image build with a Dockerfile that has a VOLUME instruction will always create a new, uniquely-named mount point on the host. Using the VOLUME instruction in a Dockerfile has somewhat limited use cases, such as when a container will run an application that will always need to read or write data that is expected at a specific location in the filesystem but should not be a part of the Union File System.

It is also possible to create a one-to-one mapping of a file on the host to a file in a container. To accomplish this, add a −v parameter to the container run command. You will need to provide the path and filename to the file to be shared from the host and the fully-qualified path to the file in the container. The container run command might look like this:

```
# Map a single file from the host to a container
echo "important data" > /tmp/data-file.txt
docker container run --rm -d \
    -v /tmp/data-file.txt:/myvol/data-file.txt \
    --name vol-demo \
    volume-demo2:1.0 tail -f /dev/null
# Prove it
docker exec vol-demo cat /myvol/data-file.txt
```

Here is what that might look like:

```
earl@ubuntu: ~/repos/dqs-samples
earl@ubuntu:~/repos/dqs-samples$ echo "important data" > /tmp/data-file.txt
earl@ubuntu:~/repos/dqs-samples$ docker container run --rm -d \
>     -v /tmp/data-file.txt:/myvol/data-file.txt \
>     --name vol-demo \
>     volume-demo2:1.0 tail -f /dev/null
0bf7782296053ae311bdc48489fe365331470b0e207873c6c5c2cc55f63d0ac4
earl@ubuntu:~/repos/dqs-samples$ docker exec vol-demo cat /myvol/data-file.txt
important data
earl@ubuntu:~/repos/dqs-samples$ █
```

There are a few different ways to define the volume in the container run command. To illustrate this point, look at the following run commands, each of which will accomplish the same thing:

```
# Using --mount with source and target
docker container run --rm -d \
    --mount source=my-volume,target=/myvol,readonly \
    --name vol-demo1 \
    volume-demo:latest tail -f /dev/null

# Using --mount with source and destination
docker container run --rm -d \
    --mount source=my-volume,destination=/myvol,readonly \
    --name vol-demo2 \
    volume-demo:latest tail -f /dev/null

# Using -v
docker container run --rm -d \
    -v my-volume:/myvol:ro \
    --name vol-demo3 \
    volume-demo:latest tail -f /dev/null
```

All three of the preceding container run commands will create a container that has mounted the same volume, in read-only mode. This can be verified with the following command:

```
# Check which container have mounted a volume by name
docker ps -a --filter volume=in-use-volume
```

```
earl@ubuntu: ~/repos/dqs-samples
earl@ubuntu:~/repos/dqs-samples$ docker ps -a --filter volume=in-use-volume
CONTAINER ID      IMAGE             COMMAND             CREATED        STATUS         PORTS      NAMES
08abdc2aafef      volume-demo2:1.0  "tail -f /dev/null"  2 minutes ago  Up 2 minutes              vol-demo3
13cf21f4e72e      volume-demo2:1.0  "tail -f /dev/null"  2 minutes ago  Up 2 minutes              vol-demo2
92e494e6bdbc      volume-demo2:1.0  "tail -f /dev/null"  3 minutes ago  Up 3 minutes              vol-demo1
earl@ubuntu:~/repos/dqs-samples$
```

References

Check out these links for more information:

- The Docker `volume create` reference: `https://docs.docker.com/engine/reference/commandline/volume_create/`
- The Docker storage reference documentation: `https://docs.docker.com/storage/`

Removing volumes

We have already seen and used the volume list command, `volume ls`, and the inspect command, `volume inspect`, and I think you should have a good grasp of what these commands do. There are two other commands in the volume-management group, both for volume removal. The first is the `volume rm` command, which you can use to remove one or more volumes by name. Then, there is the `volume prune` command; with the prune command, you can remove ALL unused volumes. Be extra careful with the use of this command. Here is the syntax for the remove and prune commands:

```
# Remove volumes command syntax
Usage: docker volume rm [OPTIONS] VOLUME [VOLUME...]
# Prune volumes command syntax
Usage: docker volume prune [OPTIONS]
```

Here are some examples of using the remove and prune commands:

```
earl@ubuntu: ~/repos/dqs-samples
earl@ubuntu:~/repos/dqs-samples$ docker volume ls
DRIVER              VOLUME NAME
local               in-use-volume
local               un-used-vol01
local               un-used-vol02
earl@ubuntu:~/repos/dqs-samples$ docker container ls
CONTAINER ID        IMAGE               COMMAND             CREATED             STATUS              PORTS               NAMES
df0fb21ee25f        volume-demo2:1.0    "tail -f /dev/null"  19 minutes ago      Up 19 minutes                           vol-demo
earl@ubuntu:~/repos/dqs-samples$ docker inspect -f '{{ range .Mounts }}{{ .Name }} {{ end }}' vol-demo
in-use-volume
earl@ubuntu:~/repos/dqs-samples$ docker volume rm un-used-vol01
un-used-vol01
earl@ubuntu:~/repos/dqs-samples$ docker volume ls
DRIVER              VOLUME NAME
local               in-use-volume
local               un-used-vol02
earl@ubuntu:~/repos/dqs-samples$ docker volume prune
WARNING! This will remove all local volumes not used by at least one container.
Are you sure you want to continue? [y/N] y
Deleted Volumes:
un-used-vol02

Total reclaimed space: 0B
```

Since the `in-use-volume` volume is mounted in the `vol-demo` container, it did not get removed with the prune command. You can use a filter on the volume list command to see what volumes are not associated with a container, and as such would be removed with the prune command. Here is the filtered ls command:

```
# Using a filter on the volume ls command
docker volume ls --filter dangling=true
```

References

Check out the following links for more information:

- Docker's Wiki document for the volume remove command: https://docs.docker.com/engine/reference/commandline/volume_rm/
- Docker's Wiki document for the volume prune command: https://docs.docker.com/engine/reference/commandline/volume_prune/
- Info on pruning Docker objects: https://docs.docker.com/config/pruning/

Sharing data between containers with data volume containers

There is another feature of Docker volumes that allows you to share the volume(s) mounted in one Docker container with other containers. It is called **data volume containers**. Using data volume containers is basically a two-step process. In the first step, you run a container that either creates or mounts Docker volumes (or both), and in the second step, you use the special volume parameter, `--volumes-from`, when running other containers to configure them to mount all of the volumes mounted in the first container. Here is an example:

```
# Step 1
docker container run \
    --rm -d \
    -v data-vol-01:/data/vol1 -v data-vol-02:/data/vol2 \
    --name data-container \
    vol-demo2:1.0 tail -f /dev/null
# Step 2
docker container run \
    --rm -d \
    --volumes-from data-container \
    --name app-container \
    vol-demo2:1.0 tail -f /dev/null
# Prove it
docker container exec app-container ls -l /data
# Prove it more
docker container inspect -f '{{ range .Mounts }}{{ .Name }} {{ end }}' app-container
```

Here is what that looks like when executed:

In this example, the first container run command is creating the volumes, but they could have just as easily been pre-created with an earlier container run command, or from a `volume create` command.

References

Here is an excellent article on data volume containers, including using them to do data backup and restore: `https://www.tricksofthetrades.net/2016/03/14/docker-data-volumes/`.

Summary

In this chapter, we took a deep-dive into Docker volumes. We learned what Docker volumes actually are, along with a few ways to create them. We learned the differences between creating Docker volumes with the `volume create` command, with the container run command, and the Dockerfile `VOLUME` instruction. We looked at a couple of ways to remove volumes, and how to use a data container to share volumes with other containers. All in all, you should feel pretty confident in your Docker volume skills right now. So far, we have built a strong base of Docker knowledge.

In `Chapter 5`, *Docker Swarm*, we are going to add to that base by learning about Docker Swarm. This is where things will really start to get exciting. If you are ready to learn more, turn the page!

5
Docker Swarm

In this chapter, we will learn what Docker swarm is, and how to set up a Docker swarm cluster. We'll learn about all of the swarm management commands, and then we will find out more about swarm managers and swarm workers. Next, we will discover swarm services. And finally, we will find out how easy it is to access a container application running on any node in a swarm cluster.

> There are currently over 17,000,000 shipping containers in the world, and 5 or 6,000,000 of them are currently shipping around the world on vessels, trucks, and trains. In total, they make around 200,000,000 trips a year.
>
> `—https://www.billiebox.co.uk/facts-about-shipping-containers`

In this chapter, we will cover the following topics:

- What is Docker swarm?
- Setting up a Docker swarm cluster
- Managers and workers
- Swarm services
- Accessing container applications in a swarm

Technical requirements

You will be pulling Docker images from Docker's public repo, so basic internet access is required to execute the examples within this chapter. You will be setting up a multi-node swarm cluster, so you will need multiple nodes to complete the examples in this chapter. You can use physical servers, EC2 instances, Virtual Machines on vSphere or Workstation or even on Virtual Box. I utilized 6 VMs on Vmware Workstation for my nodes. Each VM is configured with 1 GB ram, 1 CPU, and 20 GB HDD. The guest OS utilized is Xubuntu 18.04 for its small size and full Ubuntu feature set. Xubuntu can be downloaded from `https://xubuntu.org/download/`. Virtually any modern Linux operating system choice would be acceptable for the nodes.

The code files of this chapter can be found on GitHub:
`https://github.com/PacktPublishing/Docker-Quick-Start-Guide/tree/master/Chapter05`

Check out the following video to see the code in action:
`http://bit.ly/2KENJOD`

What is Docker swarm?

You probably have not noticed this, but so far, all of the Docker workstation deployments, or nodes that we have used in our examples have been run in single-engine mode. What does that mean? Well, it tells us that the Docker installation is managed directly and as a standalone Docker environment. While this is effective, it is not very efficient and it does not scale well. Of course, Docker understands the limitations and has provided a powerful solution to this problem. It is called Docker swarm. Docker swarm is a way to link Docker nodes together, and manage those nodes and the dockerized applications that run on them efficiently and at scale. Simply stated, a Docker swarm is a group of Docker nodes connected and managed as a cluster or swarm. Docker swarm is built into the Docker engine, so no additional installation is required to use it. When a Docker node is part of a swarm, it is running in swarm mode. If there is any doubt, you can easily check whether a system running Docker is part of a swarm or is running in single-engine mode using the `docker system info` command:

Single Engine Mode:

```
earl@ubuntu-node01:~$ docker system info | grep Swarm
Swarm: inactive
earl@ubuntu-node01:~$ ▮
```

Swarm Mode:

```
earl@ubuntu-node01:~$ docker system info | grep Swarm
Swarm: active
earl@ubuntu-node01:~$ ▮
```

The features that provide swarm mode are part of the Docker SwarmKit, which is a tool for orchestrating distributed systems at scale, that is, Docker swarm clusters. Once a Docker node joins a swarm, it becomes a swarm node, becoming either a Manager node or a Worker node. We will talk about the difference between managers and workers shortly. For now, know that the very first Docker node to join a new swarm becomes the first Manager, also known as the Leader. There is a *lot* of technical magic that happens when that first node joins a swarm (actually, it creates and initializes the swarm, and then joins it) and becomes the leader. Here is some of the wizardry that happens (in no particular order):

- A Swarm-ETCD-based configuration database or cluster store is created and encrypted
- Mutual TLS (mTLS) authentication and encryption is set up for all inter-node communication
- Container orchestration is enabled, which takes responsibility for managing which containers run on which nodes
- The cluster store is configured to automatically replicate to all manager nodes
- The node gets assigned a cryptographic ID
- A Raft-based distributed consensus-management system is enabled
- The node becomes a Manager and is elected to the status of swarm leader
- The swarm managers are configured for HA
- A public-key infrastructure system is created
- The node becomes the certificate authority, allowing it to issue client certificates to any nodes that join the swarm
- A default 90-day certificate-rotation policy is configured on the certificate authority

- The node gets issued its client certificate, which includes its name, ID, the swarm ID, and the node's role in the swarm
- Creating a new cryptographic join token for adding new swarm managers occurs
- Creating a new cryptographic join token for adding new swarm workers occurs

That list represents a lot of powerful features that you get by joining the first node to a swarm. And, with great power comes great responsibility, meaning that you really need to be prepared to do a lot of work to create your Docker swarm, as you might well imagine. So, let's move on to the next section, where we will discuss how to enable all of these features when you set up a swarm cluster.

References

Check out the following links for more information:

- The repository for SwarmKit: `https://github.com/docker/swarmkit`
- The Raft consensus algorithm: `https://raft.github.io/`

How to set up a Docker swarm cluster

You have just learned about all of the incredible features that get enabled and set up when you create a Docker swarm cluster. So, now I am going to show you all of the steps needed to set up a Docker swarm cluster. Are you ready? Here they are:

```
# Set up your Docker swarm cluster
docker swarm init
```

What? Wait? Where is the rest of it? Nope. There is nothing missing. All of the setup and functionality that is described in the preceding section is achieved with one simple command. With that single `swarm init` command, the swarm cluster is created, the node is transformed from a single-instance node into a swarm-mode node, the role of manager is assigned to the node and it is elected as the leader of the swarm, the cluster store is created, the node becomes the certificate authority of the cluster and assigns itself a new certificate that includes a cryptographic ID, a new cryptographic join token is created for managers, and another is created for workers, and on and on. This is complexity made simple.

The swarm commands make up another Docker management group. Here are the swarm-management commands:

```
earl@ubuntu-node01:~$ docker swarm --help

Usage:  docker swarm COMMAND

Manage Swarm

Commands:
  ca          Display and rotate the root CA
  init        Initialize a swarm
  join        Join a swarm as a node and/or manager
  join-token  Manage join tokens
  leave       Leave the swarm
  unlock      Unlock swarm
  unlock-key  Manage the unlock key
  update      Update the swarm

Run 'docker swarm COMMAND --help' for more information on a command.
earl@ubuntu-node01:~$
```

We'll review the purpose for each these commands in just a moment, but before we do, I want to make you aware of some important networking configurations. We will talk more about Docker networking in Chapter 6, *Docker Networking*, but for now be aware that you may need to open access to some protocols and ports on your Docker nodes to allow Docker swarm to function properly. Here is the information straight from Docker's *Getting started with swarm mode* wiki:

Open protocols and ports between the hosts

The following ports must be available. On some systems, these ports are open by default.

- **TCP port 2377** for cluster management communications
- **TCP** and **UDP port 7946** for communication among nodes
- **UDP port 4789** for overlay network traffic

If you plan on creating an overlay network with encryption (--opt encrypted), you also need to ensure **ip protocol 50 (ESP)** traffic is allowed.

Two other ports that you may need to open for the REST API are as follows:

- TCP 2375 for Docker REST API (plain text)
- TCP 2376 for Docker REST API (ssl)

Alright, let's move on to reviewing the swarm commands.

docker swarm init

You have already seen what the init command is for, that being to create the swarm cluster, add (this) the first Docker node to it, and then set up and enable all of the swarm features we just covered. The init command can be as simple as using it with no parameters, but there are many optional parameters available to fine-tune the initialization process. You can get a full list of the optional parameters, as usual, by using `--help`, but let's consider a few of the available parameters now:

- `--autolock`: Use this parameter to enable manager autolocking.
- `--cert-expiry duration`: Use this parameter to change the default validity period (of 90 days) for node certificates.
- `--external-ca external-ca`: Use this parameter to specify one or more certificate-signing endpoints, that is, external CAs.

docker swarm join-token

When you initialize the swarm by running the `swarm init` command on the first node, one of the functions that is executed creates unique cryptographic join tokens, one joins additional manager nodes, and one joins worker nodes. Using the `join-token` command, you can obtain these two join tokens. In fact, using the `join-token` command will deliver the full join command for whichever role you specify. The role parameter is required. Here are examples of the command:

```
# Get the join token for adding managers
docker swarm join-token manager
# Get the join token for adding workers
docker swarm join-token worker
```

Here is what that looks like:

```
earl@ubuntu-node01:~$ docker swarm join-token manager
To add a manager to this swarm, run the following command:

    docker swarm join --token SWMTKN-1-3ovu7fbnqfqlw66csvvfw5xgljl26mdv0dudcdssjdcltk2sen-a830t
v7e8bajxu1k5dc0045zn 192.168.159.156:2377

earl@ubuntu-node01:~$ docker swarm join-token worker
To add a worker to this swarm, run the following command:

    docker swarm join --token SWMTKN-1-3ovu7fbnqfqlw66csvvfw5xgljl26mdv0dudcdssjdcltk2sen-5bjqn
dakci6tas05nny2hwhc2 192.168.159.156:2377

earl@ubuntu-node01:~$ █
```

```
# Rotate the worker join token
docker swarm join-token --rotate worker
```

Note that this does not invalidate existing workers that have used the old, now invalid, join token. They are still a part of the swarm and are unaffected by the change in the join token. Only new nodes that you wish to join to the swarm need to use the new token.

docker swarm join

You have already seen the join command used in the preceding *docker swarm join-token* section. The join command is used, in conjunction with a cryptographic join token, to add a Docker node to the swarm. All nodes except the very first node will use the join command to become part of the swarm (the first node uses the "init" command, of course). The join command has a few parameters, the most important of them being the `--token` parameter. This is the required join token, obtainable with the `join-token` command. Here is an example:

```
# Join this node to an existing swarm
docker swarm join --token
SWMTKN-1-3ovu7fbnqfqlw66csvvfw5xgljl26mdv0dudcdssjdcltk2sen-
a830tv7e8bajxu1k5dc0045zn 192.168.159.156:2377
```

You will notice that the role is not needed for this command. This is because the token itself is associated with the role it has been created for. When you execute the join, the output provides an informational message telling you what role the node has joined as manager or worker. If you have inadvertently use a manager token to join a worker or vice versa, you can use the `leave` command to remove a node from the swarm, and then using the token for the actual desired role, rejoin the node to the swarm.

docker swarm ca

The `swarm ca` command is used when you want to view the current certificate for the swarm, or you need to rotate the current swarm certificate. To rotate the certificate, you would include the `--rotate` parameter:

```
# View the current swarm certificate
docker swarm ca
# Rotate the swarm certificate
docker swarm ca --rotate
```

The `swarm ca` command can only be executed successfully on a swarm manager node. One reason you might use the rotate swarm certificate feature is if you are moving from the internal root CA to an external CA, or vice versa. Another reason you might need to rotate the swarm certificate is in the event of one or more manager nodes getting compromised. In that case, rotating the swarm certificate will block all other managers from being able to communicate with the manager that rotated the certificate or each other using the old certificate. When you rotate the certificate, the command will remain active, blocking until all swarm nodes, both managers and workers, have been updated. Here is an example of rotating the certificate on a very small cluster:

```
earl@ubuntu-node01:~$ docker swarm ca --rotate
desired root digest: sha256:2ee684265b796efe340f42e6353a200e1d62b9c4d0d2627ac7428deb6e966af3
   rotated TLS certificates:   [==================================================>] 4/4 nodes
   rotated CA certificates:    [==================================================>] 4/4 nodes
-----BEGIN CERTIFICATE-----
MIIBajCCARCgAwIBAgIUHOGNLx2R3wwcRElIHigrWgNmOnEwCgYIKoZIzj0EAwIw
EzERMA8GA1UEAxMIc3dhcm0tY2EwHhcNMTgwOTE5MDE0OTAwWhcNMzgwOTE0MDE0
OTAwWjATMREwDwYDVQQDEwhzd2FybS1jYTBZMBMGByqGSM49AgEGCCqGSM49AwEH
A0IABC9IQowItYlcMTzRPiCMx7vWRJomKei/l8D2duSf6gNOOnDmZh/1cFeQ1uS6
8tL1FOm5DRd3+AIF4PxhX9GfYlSjQjBAMA4GA1UdDwEB/wQEAwIBBjAPBgNVHRMB
Af8EBTADAQH/MB0GA1UdDgQWBBSOik9ARb8STCuqGiPtz6KEN19fqDAKBggqhkjO
PQQDAgNIADBFAiANcHR07RamLhq5zX+YJpMa8cIO+Pt6/mCrfnMZvIIdZAIhAKUh
rmWkM70UXsbZ4Z8A4Gbufu7BxxFWrhlXHKoYAb64
-----END CERTIFICATE-----
earl@ubuntu-node01:~$ 
```

Since the command will remain active until all nodes have updated both the TLS certificate and the CA certificate, it can present an issue if there are nodes in the swarm that are offline. When that is a potential problem, you can include the `--detach` parameter, and the command will initiate the certificate rotation and return control immediately to the session. Be aware that you will not get any status as to the progress, success, or failure of the certificate rotation when you use the `--detach` optional parameter. You can use the node ls command to query the state of the certificates within the cluster to check the progress. Here is the full command you can use:

```
# Query the state of the certificate rotation in a swarm cluster
docker node ls --format '{{.ID}} {{.Hostname}} {{.Status}} {{.TLSStatus}}'
```

The `ca rotate` command will continue trying to complete, either in the foreground, or in the background if detached. If a node was offline when the rotate is initiated, and it comes back online, the certificate rotation will complete. Here is an example of `node04` being offline when the rotate command was executed, and then a while later, after it came back on; check the status found it successfully rotated:

```
earl@ubuntu-node01:~$ docker swarm ca --rotate --detach
earl@ubuntu-node01:~$ docker node ls --format '{{.ID}} {{.Hostname}} {{.Status}} {{.TLSStatus}}'
t854pp446aqgluukathc4ympo ubuntu-node01 Ready Ready
wltmsmeijvjyi8b2429twv3sd ubuntu-node02 Ready Ready
chqi3oq7jrulps39jxot2hju0 ubuntu-node03 Ready Ready
0x917r93bji0bitokh129uowx ubuntu-node04 Down Needs Rotation
earl@ubuntu-node01:~$ docker node ls --format '{{.ID}} {{.Hostname}} {{.Status}} {{.TLSStatus}}'
t854pp446aqgluukathc4ympo ubuntu-node01 Ready Ready
wltmsmeijvjyi8b2429twv3sd ubuntu-node02 Ready Ready
chqi3oq7jrulps39jxot2hju0 ubuntu-node03 Ready Ready
0x917r93bji0bitokh129uowx ubuntu-node04 Ready Ready
earl@ubuntu-node01:~$ 
```

Another important point to remember is that rotating the certificate will immediately invalidate both of the current join tokens.

docker swarm unlock

You may recall from the discussion regarding the `docker swarm init` command that one of the optional parameters that you can include with the `init` command is `--autolock`. Using this parameter will enable the autolock feature on the swarm cluster. What does that mean? Well, when a swarm cluster is configured to use auto-locking, any time the docker daemon of a manager node goes offline, and then comes back online (that is, is restarted) it is necessary to enter an unlock key to allow the node to rejoin the swarm. Why would you use the auto-lock feature to lock your swarm? The auto-lock feature helps to protect the mutual TLS encryption key of the swarm, along with the encrypt and decrypt keys used with the swarm's raft logs. It is an additional security feature intended to supplement Docker Secrets. When the docker daemon restarts on the manager node of a locked swarm, you must enter the unlock key. Here is what using the unlock key looks like:

```
earl@ubuntu-node03:~$ sudo service docker restart
[sudo] password for earl:
earl@ubuntu-node03:~$ docker node ls
Error response from daemon: Swarm is encrypted and needs to be unlocked before it can be used. Please use "docker swarm unlock" to unlock it.
earl@ubuntu-node03:~$ docker swarm unlock
Please enter unlock key:
earl@ubuntu-node03:~$ docker node ls
ID                        HOSTNAME         STATUS      AVAILABILITY      MANAGER STATUS      ENGINE VERSION
t854pp446aqg1uukathc4ympo ubuntu-node01    Ready       Active          t Leader             18.06.1-ce
```

By the way, to the rest of the swarm, a manager node that has not been unlocked will report as down, even though the docker daemon is running. The swarm auto-lock feature can be enabled or disabled on an existing swarm cluster using the `swarm update` command, which we will take a look at shortly. The unlock key is generated during the swarm initialization and will be presented on the command line at that time. If you have lost the unlock key, you can retrieve it on an unlocked manager node using the `swarm unlock-key` command.

docker swarm unlock-key

The `swarm unlock-key` command is much like the `swarm ca` command. The unlock-key command can be used to retrieve the current swarm unlock key, or it can be used to rotate the unlock key to a new one:

```
# Retrieve the current unlock key
docker swarm unlock-key
# Rotate to a new unlock key
docker swarm unlock-key --rotate
```

Depending on the size of the swarm cluster, the unlock key rotation can take a while for all of the manager nodes to get updated.

It is a good idea to keep the current (old) key handy for a while when you rotate the unlock key, on the off-chance that a manager node goes offline before getting the updated key. That way, you can still unlock the node using the old key. Once the node is unlocked and receives the rotated (new) unlock key, the old key can be discarded.

As you might expect, the `swarm unlock-key` command is only useful when issued on a manager node of a cluster with the auto-lock feature enabled. If you have a cluster that does not have the auto-lock feature enabled, you can enable it with the `swarm update` command.

docker swarm update

There are several swarm cluster features that are enabled or configured when you initialize the cluster on the first manager node via the `docker swarm init` command. There may be times that you want to change which features are enabled, disabled, or configured after the cluster has been initialized. To accomplish this, you will need to use the `swarm update` command. For example, you may want to enable the auto-lock feature for your swarm cluster. Or, you might want to change the length of time that certificates are valid for. These are the types of changes you can execute using the `swarm update` command. Doing so might look like this:

```
# Enable autolock on your swarm cluster
docker swarm update --autolock=true
# Adjust certificate expiry to 30 days
docker swarm update --cert-expiry 720h
```

Here is the list of settings that can be affected by the `swarm update` command:

```
earl@ubuntu-node01:~$ docker swarm update --help

Usage:  docker swarm update [OPTIONS]

Update the swarm

Options:
      --autolock                        Change manager autolocking setting (true|false)
      --cert-expiry duration            Validity period for node certificates (ns|us|ms|s|m|h) (default 2160h0m0s)
      --dispatcher-heartbeat duration   Dispatcher heartbeat period (ns|us|ms|s|m|h) (default 5s)
      --external-ca external-ca         Specifications of one or more certificate signing endpoints
      --max-snapshots uint              Number of additional Raft snapshots to retain
      --snapshot-interval uint          Number of log entries between Raft snapshots (default 10000)
      --task-history-limit int          Task history retention limit (default 5)
earl@ubuntu-node01:~$
```

docker swarm leave

This one is pretty much what you would expect. You can remove a docker node from a swarm with the `leave` command. Here is an example of needing to use the `leave` command to correct a user error:

```
earl@ubuntu-node03:~$ docker system info | grep Swarm
Swarm: inactive
earl@ubuntu-node03:~$ docker swarm join --token SWMTKN-1-10qhnx62raze9h2otsw0uri44gon7juh0w1g658m7h1pxfvrqi-4rbpdo3
1xj0all7lplwlwe120 192.168.159.156:2377
This node joined a swarm as a worker.
earl@ubuntu-node03:~$ docker system info | grep Swarm
Swarm: active
earl@ubuntu-node03:~$ #opps, I wanted node3 to join as a manager
earl@ubuntu-node03:~$ docker swarm leave
Node left the swarm.
earl@ubuntu-node03:~$ docker system info | grep Swarm
Swarm: inactive
earl@ubuntu-node03:~$ docker swarm join --token SWMTKN-1-10qhnx62raze9h2otsw0uri44gon7juh0w1g658m7h1pxfvrqi-93qaiep
0lcbl6v9vor39oseft 192.168.159.156:2377
This node joined a swarm as a manager.
earl@ubuntu-node03:~$ docker system info | grep Swarm
Swarm: active
earl@ubuntu-node03:~$ ▮
```

Node03 was intended to be a manager node. I accidentally added the node as a worker. Realizing my error, I used the `swarm leave` command to remove the node from the swarm, putting it back into single instance mode. Then, using the *manager* join token, I re-added the node to the swarm as a manager. Phew! Crisis averted.

References

Check out these links for more information:

- Getting started with swarm mode tutorial: `https://docs.docker.com/engine/swarm/swarm-tutorial/`
- The `docker swarm init` command wiki doc: `https://docs.docker.com/engine/reference/commandline/swarm_init/`
- The `docker swarm ca` command wiki doc: `https://docs.docker.com/engine/reference/commandline/swarm_ca/`
- The `docker swarm join-token` command wiki doc: `https://docs.docker.com/engine/reference/commandline/swarm_join-token/`

- The `docker swarm join` **command wiki doc:** `https://docs.docker.com/engine/reference/commandline/swarm_join/`
- The `docker swarm unlock` **command wiki doc:** `https://docs.docker.com/engine/reference/commandline/swarm_unlock/`
- The `docker swarm unlock-key` **command wiki doc:** `https://docs.docker.com/engine/reference/commandline/swarm_unlock-key/`
- The `docker swarm update` **command wiki doc:** `https://docs.docker.com/engine/reference/commandline/swarm_update/`
- The `docker swarm leave` **command wiki doc:** `https://docs.docker.com/engine/reference/commandline/swarm_leave/`
- **Learn more about Docker Secrets:** `https://docs.docker.com/engine/swarm/secrets/`

Managers and workers

We have discussed swarm managers a little in the previous sections, but let's take a closer look at what swarm managers do. The swarm managers do exactly what you would expect. They manage and maintain the state of the swarm cluster. They schedule swarm services, which we will talk about in *Swarm services* section of this chapter, but for now, think of swarm services as running containers. Manager nodes also serve up the API endpoints of the cluster, allowing for programmatic access via REST. Managers also direct traffic to the running services so that any container can be reached through any manager node without having to know which node is actually running the containers. As part of maintaining the state of the cluster, the managers will deal with the loss of nodes in the system, electing a new leader node in the event that the manager lost was the leader, and they will keep the desired number of service containers running if containers or nodes go down.

The best practices for the number of manager in a swarm are three, five, or seven. You'll note that all of these options represent an odd number of manager nodes. This is so that if the leader node is lost, the raft consensus algorithm can more easily select a new leader for the swarm. You can run a swarm cluster with one manager node, and that is actually a better option than having two manager nodes. But, for a much more highly available swarm cluster, it is recommended that you have at least three manager nodes. For larger clusters, having five or seven managers is good, but it is not recommended to have more than seven. Once you have more than seven managers in the same cluster, you actually experience degraded performance.

Another important consideration for the manager nodes is the network performance between them. Managers need a low-latency network connection for optimal performance. If you are running your swarm in AWS, for example, you probably don't want the managers within a swarm spread across regions. You would likely encounter issues with the swarm if you were to do so. If you put the managers within a swarm in different availability zones within a single region, you shouldn't have any network-performance-related issues.

Worker nodes don't do anything except run containers. They don't have a say in electing new leaders when the leader node goes down. They don't handle API calls. They don't direct traffic. They do nothing but run containers. In fact, you can't have a swarm with just a worker node. On the other hand, you can have a swarm with just a manager node, in which case the manager will also act as a worker and run containers in addition to its manager duties.

All manager nodes are actually worker nodes as well by default. This means that they can and will run containers. If you want to keep your managers from running workloads, you need to change the node's availability setting. Changing it to draining will carefully stop any running containers on the manager node marked as draining, and will start up those containers on other (non-draining) nodes. No new container workloads will be started on a node in drain mode, for example as follows:

```
# Set node03's availability to drain
docker node update --availability drain ubuntu-node03
```

There may be times when you want or need to change the role of a docker node in the swarm. You can promote a worker node to manager status, or you can demote a manager node to worker status. Here are some examples of these activities:

```
# Promote worker nodes 04 and 05 to manager status
docker node promote ubuntu-node04 ubuntu-node05
# Demote manager nodes 01 and 02 to worker status
docker node demote ubuntu-node01 ubuntu-node02
```

References

Check out the official documentation on how nodes work at https://docs.docker.com/engine/swarm/how-swarm-mode-works/nodes/.

Swarm services

Alright. Now you know a lot about setting up a Docker swarm cluster, and how its nodes go from single-engine mode into swarm mode. You also know that the significance of that is to free you from directly managing individual running containers. So, you may be starting to wonder, if I don't manage my containers directly and individually now, how do I manage them? You've come to the right place! This is where swarm services come into play. swarm services allow you to define the desired state for your container application in terms of how many concurrent running copies of the container there should be. Let's take a quick look at what commands are available to us in the management group for swarm services, and then we'll talk about those commands:

```
earl@ubuntu-node01:~$ docker service --help

Usage:  docker service COMMAND

Manage services

Commands:
  create     Create a new service
  inspect    Display detailed information on one or more services
  logs       Fetch the logs of a service or task
  ls         List services
  ps         List the tasks of one or more services
  rm         Remove one or more services
  rollback   Revert changes to a service's configuration
  scale      Scale one or multiple replicated services
  update     Update a service

Run 'docker service COMMAND --help' for more information on a command.
earl@ubuntu-node01:~$
```

The first thing that you'll probably want to do is create a new service, so we will begin our swarm services discussion with the `service create` command. Here is the syntax and a basic sample of the `service create` command:

```
# Syntax for the service create command
# Usage: docker service create [OPTIONS] IMAGE [COMMAND] [ARG...]
# Create a service
docker service create --replicas 1 --name submarine alpine ping google.com
```

OK. Let's break down the sample `service create` command shown here. First, you have the management group service followed by the `create` command. Then, we start getting into the parameters; the first one is `--replicas`. This defines the number of copies of the container that should be run concurrently. Next, we have the `--name` parameter. This one is pretty obvious and is the name of the service we are creating, in this case, `submarine`. We will be able to use the stated name in other service commands. After the name parameter, we have the fully-qualified Docker image name. In this case, it is just `alpine`. It could have been something such as `alpine:3.8`, or `alpine:latest`, or something more qualified such as `tenstartups/alpine:latest`. Following the image name to use for the service is the command to use when running the container and the parameters to pass to that command—`ping` and `google.com`, respectively. So, the preceding sample `service create` command will launch a single container from the `alpine` image, which will run the `ping` command with the google.com parameter, and then name the service `submarine`. Here is what that looks like:

```
earl@ubuntu-node01:~$ docker service create --replicas 1 --name submarine alpine ping google.com
q3nch2rpr7hag8vmr3mxltvfp
overall progress: 1 out of 1 tasks
1/1: running  [==================================================>]
verify: Service converged
earl@ubuntu-node01:~$ 
```

You now know the basics of creating docker services. But, before you get too excited, there's still a lot of ground to cover for the `service create` command. In fact, this command has so many options that listing them all out would take two pages in this book. So, rather than do that, I want you to use the `--help` feature and enter the following command now:

```
# Get help with the service create command
docker service create --help
```

I know, right? There are a *lot* of optional parameters you can use. Don't worry. I'm not going to leave you out to dry here. I'll give you some guidance to help you get a firm foundation for creating services, and then you can branch out and try some of the other parameters you see in `--help`.

Just so you know, the two parameters we used so far, `--replicas` and `--name`, are both optional. If you don't provide a number of replicas to use, the service will be created with a default of 1. Also, if you don't provide a name for the service, a fanciful name will be made up and given to the service. This is the same type of default naming we saw when using the `docker container run` command in Chapter 2, *Learning Docker Commands*. It is generally better to provide both of these options for each `service create` command issued.

Also, know that generally speaking, the command and command parameters for the image that were supplied in the preceding sample are optional as well. In this specific case, they are necessary because, by itself, a container run from the alpine image with no other command or parameters supplied will just exit. In the sample, that would show up as a failure to converge the service and Docker would perpetually try to restart the service. Stated another way, you can leave off the command and its parameters if the image being used has them built in (such as in the CMD or ENTRYPOINT instruction of the Dockerfile).

Let's move on to some more create parameters now. You should recall from Chapter 2, *Learning Docker Commands* that there is a `--publish` parameter you can use on a `docker container run` command that defines the port exposed on the docker host and the port in the container that the host port is mapped to. It looked something like this:

```
# Create a nginx web-server that redirects host traffic from port 8080 to
port 80 in the container
docker container run --detach --name web-server1 --publish 8080:80 nginx
```

Well, you need the same functionality for a swarm service, and in their wisdom, Docker made the parameter used for both the `container run` command and the `service create` command the same: `--publish`. You can use the same abbreviated format we saw before, `--publish 8080:80`, or you can use a more verbose format: `--publish published=8080,target=80`. This still translates to redirect host traffic from port 8080 to port 80 in the container. Let's try out another example, this time one that uses the `--publish` parameter. We'll give the nginx image another run:

```
# Create a nginx web-server service using the publish parameter
docker service create --name web-service --replicas 3 --publish
published=8080,target=80 nginx
```

This example will create a new service that runs three container replicas, using the `nginx` image and exposing port `80` on the containers and port `8080` on the hosts. Have a look:

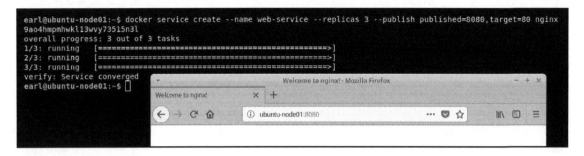

Now, you're getting there. Let's quickly cover three more parameters and you will be ready to take on the world (of swarm services, at least). First up, `--restart-window`. This parameter is used to tell the Docker daemon how long to wait for the container to start up its application before testing to see whether it is healthy. The default is five seconds. If you create an app in your container that will take more than five seconds to start up and report as healthy, you will want to include a `--restart-window` parameter with your `service create`. Next up, `--restart-max-attempts`. This parameter tells the Docker daemon how many times to keep trying to start a container replica that is not reporting as healthy before giving up. The default is *Never give up. Never surrender!* Finally, let's talk about the `--mode` parameter. The default mode for a swarm service is *replicated*. That means the Docker daemon will continue to stand up containers for your service until the number of concurrently running containers is equal to the value you provided in the `--replicas` parameter (or 1 if you don't provide the parameter). For example, with a `--replicas 3` parameter, you will get three containers running in the swarm for your service. There is another mode, called **global**. If you provide the `--mode global` parameter when you create your service, the Docker daemon will stand up exactly one container on every node in the cluster. If you have a six-node cluster, you will end up with six containers running, one per node. With a 12-node cluster, you get 12 containers, and so on. This is a very handy option when you have services that provide functionality for each host, such as a monitoring app or log forwarder.

Let's review some of the other service commands you will want to know and use. Once you've created some services, you might want a list of those services. This can be achieved with the `service list` command. It looks like this:

```
# List services in the swarm
# Usage: docker service ls [OPTIONS]
docker service list
```

Once you have reviewed the list of running services, you might want more details about one or more of those services. To achieve this, you would use the `service ps` command. Have a look:

```
# List the tasks associated with a service
# Usage: docker service ps [OPTIONS] SERVICE [SERVICE...]
docker service ps
```

Once a service has outlived its usefulness, you might want to terminate it. The command to do that is the `service remove` command. Here is what that looks like:

```
# Remove one or more services from the swarm
# Usage: docker service rm SERVICE [SERVICE...]
docker service remove sleepy_snyder
```

If you want to remove all of the services running in the swarm, you can combine some of these commands and execute something such as this:

```
# Remove ALL the services from the swarm
docker service remove $(docker service list -q)
```

Finally, if you realize that the number of replicas currently configured is not set to the desired number, you can use the `service scale` command to adjust it. Here is how you do that:

```
# Adjust the configured number of replicas for a service
# Usage: docker service scale SERVICE=REPLICAS [SERVICE=REPLICAS...]
docker service scale web-service=4
```

```
earl@ubuntu-node01:~$ docker service ls
ID              NAME            MODE            REPLICAS    IMAGE           PORTS
lm68g70ar8ci    confident_cori  replicated      1/1         alpine:latest
zp4u6riel5pg    sleepy_snyder   replicated      1/1         alpine:latest
t1etenue72p6    submarine       replicated      1/1         alpine:latest
9ao4hmpmhwkl    web-service     replicated      3/3         nginx:latest    *:8080->80/tcp
earl@ubuntu-node01:~$ docker service ps web-service
ID              NAME            IMAGE           NODE            DESIRED STATE   CURRENT STATE
yqh8tvuzpshk    web-service.1   nginx:latest    ubuntu-node01   Running         Running 11 hours ago
4345t4poy83r    \_ web-service.1 nginx:latest   ubuntu-node04   Shutdown        Shutdown 11 hours ago
wqv78x9r3qvx    web-service.3   nginx:latest    ubuntu-node02   Running         Running 21 hours ago
olqytmgegzdn    web-service.4   nginx:latest    ubuntu-node04   Running         Running 55 seconds ago
earl@ubuntu-node01:~$ docker service rm sleepy_snyder
sleepy_snyder
earl@ubuntu-node01:~$ docker service scale web-service=4
web-service scaled to 4
overall progress: 4 out of 4 tasks
1/4: running    [==========================================>]
2/4: running    [==========================================>]
3/4: running    [==========================================>]
4/4: running    [==========================================>]
verify: Service converged
earl@ubuntu-node01:~$
```

That should be enough to keep you busy for a while. Before we move on Chapter 6, *Docker Networking*, let's cover one more topic in this chapter: accessing your container applications running in a swarm.

References

Read more about the Docker service create reference at https://docs.docker.com/engine/reference/commandline/service_create/.

Accessing container applications in a swarm

So, now you have a swarm running with an odd number of manager nodes, and a number of worker nodes. You have deployed some swarm services to run your favorite containerized applications. What's next? Well, you just might want to access one or more of the applications running in your swarm. Perhaps you have deployed a web server application. It would be nice to be able to visit the web pages shared by that web server, right? Let's take a quick look and see how easy it is to do so.

One of the features that the swarm managers handle for us is to direct traffic to our services. In an earlier example, we set up a web service that was running three replicas in the swarm. The swarm I am currently using happens to have three manager nodes and three worker nodes. All six nodes are eligible to run workloads so when the service is started, three of the six nodes will end up running a container. If we take a look at the details of the tasks of the service using the `service ps` command, you can see which of the six nodes are running the web-service containers:

```
earl@ubuntu-node01:~$ docker service ps web-service
ID                NAME            IMAGE           NODE            DESIRED STATE    CURRENT STATE
kh7vvjzc6qrg      web-service.1   nginx:latest    ubuntu-node01   Running          Running 21 seconds ago
6dmzivr2dzee      web-service.2   nginx:latest    ubuntu-node02   Running          Running 20 seconds ago
eqg00r47n7qp      web-service.3   nginx:latest    ubuntu-node04   Running          Running 22 seconds ago
earl@ubuntu-node01:~$
```

In this example, you can see that the web service containers are running on node 01, 02, and 04. The wonderful thing is that you don't need to know which nodes are running your service containers. You can access the service via any node in the swarm. Of course, you would expect to be able to access the container on node 01, 02, or 04, but have a look at this:

There is an unfortunate side-effect of having the ability to access a service from any node in the swarm. Can you think of what it might be? I won't keep you in suspense for long. The side effect is that you can only assign a (host) port to one service in the swarm. In our example, we are using port 8080 for our web service. That means that we cannot use port 8080 for the host port of any other service we want to run in this swarm:

```
earl@ubuntu-node01:~$ docker service create --name new-web-service --replicas 3 --publish published=8080,target=80 nginx
Error response from daemon: rpc error: code = InvalidArgument desc = port '8080' is already in use by service 'web-service' (kt
) as an ingress port
earl@ubuntu-node01:~$
```

References

Check out the following links for more information:

- Wiki doc with a very detailed overview of deploying services on a swarm: https://docs.docker.com/v17.09/engine/swarm/services/
- How services work: https://docs.docker.com/engine/swarm/how-swarm-mode-works/services/
- Docker's getting started with swarm mode training: https://docs.docker.com/v17.09/engine/swarm/swarm-tutorial/

Summary

In this chapter, we finally started to pull some of the pieces together and make some fun stuff happen. We learned how much functionality we get by enabling swarm mode, and creating a swarm cluster. And, we found out just how easy it is to set everything up, using one single `swarm init` command. Then, we learned how to grow and manage our swarm cluster, and finally, we learned how to run our containers as services within our new swarm cluster. It's been fun, right?!

Now, let's take things to the next level. In `Chapter 6`, *Docker Networking*, we'll learn about Docker Networking. If you're ready for more good stuff, turn the page.

6
Docker Networking

In this chapter, we will learn about Docker networking. We will dive deep into Docker networking, learning how containers can be isolated, how they can communicate with each other, and how they can communicate with the outside world. We will explore the local network drivers Docker provides in the out-of-the-box installation. Then, we will examine the use of remote network drivers with an example deployment of the Weave driver. After that, we will learn how to create Docker networks. We will round out the discussion with a look at the free services that we get with our Docker networks.

> *"Approximately 97% of all shipping containers are manufactured in China. It is far easier to produce the container close to the shipment than to re-position containers around the world."*

> — https://www.billiebox.co.uk/

In this chapter, we will cover the following topics:

- What is a Docker network?
- What built-in (also known as **local**) Docker networks are all about
- What about third-party (also known as **remote**) Docker networks?
- How to create Docker networks
- The free service discovery and load balancing features
- The right Docker network driver to use for your needs

Technical requirements

You will be pulling Docker images from Docker's public repo, and installing network drivers from Weave, so basic internet access is required to execute the examples within this chapter. Also, we will be using the `jq software` package, so if you haven't installed it yet, please see the instructions on how to do so—they can be found in *The container inspect command* section of `Chapter 2`, *Learning Docker Commands*.

The code files of this chapter can be found on GitHub:
`https://github.com/PacktPublishing/Docker-Quick-Start-Guide/tree/master/Chapter06`

Check out the following video to see the code in action:
`http://bit.ly/2FJ2iBK`

What is a Docker network?

As you already know, a network is a linkage system that allows computers and other hardware devices to communicate. A Docker network is the same thing. It is a linkage system that allows Docker containers to communicate with each other on the same Docker host, or with containers, computers, and hardware outside of the container's host, including containers running on other Docker hosts.

If you are familiar with the cloud computing analogy of pets versus cattle, you understand the necessity of being able to manage resources at scale. Docker networks allow you to do just that. They abstract away most of the complexity of networking, delivering easy-to-understand, easy-to-document, and easy-to-use networks for your containerized apps. The Docker network is based on a standard, created by Docker, called the **Container Network Model (CNM)**. There is a competing networking standard, created by CoreOS, called the **Container Network Interface (CNI)**. The CNI standard has been adopted by several projects, most notably Kubernetes, and arguments can be made to support its use. However, in this chapter, we will focus our attention on the CNM standard from Docker.

The CNM has been implemented by the libnetwork project, and you can learn more about that project by following the link in the references for this section. The CNM implementation, written in Go, is made up of three constructs: the sandbox, the endpoint, and the network. The sandbox is a network namespace. Each container has its own sandbox. It holds the configuration of the container's network stack. This includes its routing tables, interfaces, and DNS settings for IP and MAC addresses. The sandbox also contains the network endpoints for the container. Next, the endpoints are what join the sandbox to networks. Endpoints are essentially network interfaces, such as **eth0**. A container's sandbox may have more than one endpoint, but each endpoint will connect to only a single network. Finally, a network is a collection of connected endpoints, which allow communication between connections. Every network has a name, an address space, an ID, and a network type.

Libnetwork is a pluggable architecture that allows network drivers to implement the specifics for the components we just described. Each network type has its own network driver. Docker provides built-in drivers. These default, or local, drivers include the bridge driver and the overlay driver. In addition to the built-in drivers, libnetwork supports third-party-created drivers. These drivers are referred to as remote drivers. Some examples of remote drivers include Calico, Contiv, and Weave.

You now know a little about what a Docker network is, and after reading these details, you might be thinking, where's the *easy* that he talked about? Hang in there. now we are going to start discussing how easy it is for you to create and use Docker networks. As with Docker volume, the network commands represent their own management category. As you would expect, the top-level management command for network is as follows:

```
# Docker network managment command
docker network
```

The subcommands available in the network management group include the following:

```
# Docker network management subcommands
docker network connect          # Connect a container to a network
docker network create           # Create a network
docker network disconnect       # Disconnect a container from a network
docker network inspect          # Display network details
docker network ls               # List networks
docker network rm               # Remove one or more networks
docker network prune            # Remove all unused networks
```

Let's now take a look at the built-in or local network drivers.

References

Check out the following links for more information:

- Pets versus cattle talk slide-deck: `https://www.slideshare.net/randybias/architectures-for-open-and-scalable-clouds`
- Libnetwork project: `https://github.com/docker/libnetwork`
- Libnetwork design: `https://github.com/docker/libnetwork/blob/master/docs/design.md`
- Calico network driver: `https://www.projectcalico.org/`
- Contiv network driver: `http://contiv.github.io/`
- Weave network driver: `https://www.weave.works/docs/net/latest/overview/`

Built-in (local) Docker networks

The out-of-the-box install of Docker includes a few built-in network drivers. These are also known as local drivers. The two most commonly used drivers are the bridge network driver and the overlay network driver. Other built-in drivers include none, host, and MACVLAN. Also, without your creating networks, your fresh install will have a few networks pre-created and ready to use. Using the `network ls` command, we can easily see the list of pre-created networks available in the fresh installation:

```
earl@ubuntu-node01:~$ docker network ls
NETWORK ID          NAME                DRIVER              SCOPE
32a527a0ec19        bridge              bridge              local
7245a5bfc80c        host                host                local
73643f1d3b6a        none                null                local
earl@ubuntu-node01:~$
```

In this list, you will notice that each network has its unique ID, a name, a driver used to create it (and that controls it), and a network scope. Don't confuse a scope of local with the category of driver, which is also local. The local category is used to differentiate the driver's origin from third-party drivers that have a category of remote. A scope value of local indicates that the limit of communication for the network is bound to within the local Docker host. To clarify, if two Docker hosts, H1 and H2, both contain a network that has the scope of local, containers on H1 will never be able to communicate directly with containers on H2, even if they use the same driver and the networks have the same name. The other scope value is swarm, which we'll talk more about shortly.

 The pre-created networks that are found in all deployments of Docker are special in that they cannot be removed. It is not necessary to attach containers to any of them, but attempts to remove them with the `docker network rm` command will always result in an error.

There are three built-in network drivers that have a scope of local: bridge, host, and none. The host network driver leverages the networking stack of the Docker host, essentially bypassing the networking of Docker. All containers on the host network are able to communicate with each other through the host's interfaces. A significant limitation to using the host network driver is that each port can only be used by a single container. That is, for example, you cannot run two nginx containers that are both bound to port 80. As you may have guessed because the host driver leverages the network of the host it is running on, each Docker host can only have one network using the host driver:

```
earl@ubuntu-node01:~$ docker container run -d --network host --name container-host-net alpine tail -f /dev/null
79b72a2cf2c608fb2ebe367147269a16de51b38a8bd850268eb24ede05ccbb6c
earl@ubuntu-node01:~$ docker container exec -it container-host-net ifconfig
docker0    Link encap:Ethernet  HWaddr 02:42:8C:0C:CB:A8
           inet addr:172.17.0.1  Bcast:172.17.255.255  Mask:255.255.0.0
           UP BROADCAST MULTICAST  MTU:1500  Metric:1
           RX packets:0 errors:0 dropped:0 overruns:0 frame:0
           TX packets:0 errors:0 dropped:0 overruns:0 carrier:0
           collisions:0 txqueuelen:0
           RX bytes:0 (0.0 B)  TX bytes:0 (0.0 B)

docker_gwbridge Link encap:Ethernet  HWaddr 02:42:0B:79:A7:3E
           inet addr:172.21.0.1  Bcast:172.21.255.255  Mask:255.255.0.0
           inet6 addr: fe80::42:bff:fe79:a73e/64 Scope:Link
           UP BROADCAST RUNNING MULTICAST  MTU:1500  Metric:1
           RX packets:0 errors:0 dropped:0 overruns:0 frame:0
           TX packets:67 errors:0 dropped:0 overruns:0 carrier:0
           collisions:0 txqueuelen:0
           RX bytes:0 (0.0 B)  TX bytes:7562 (7.3 KiB)

ens33      Link encap:Ethernet  HWaddr 00:0C:29:56:9F:94
           inet addr:192.168.159.156  Bcast:192.168.159.255  Mask:255.255.255.0
           inet6 addr: fe80::cc57:5d72:7d02:f732/64 Scope:Link
```

Next up, is the null or none network. Using the null network driver creates a network that when a container is connected to it provides a full network stack but does not configure any interfaces within the container. This renders the container completely isolated. This driver is provided mainly for backward-compatibility purposes, and like the host driver, only one network of the null type can be created on a Docker host:

```
earl@ubuntu-node01:~$ docker container run -d --network none --name container-null-net alpine tail -f /dev/null
8adefa72b20932142bf160dc6defd1fe424f071d84c7e78079f797bca460acde
earl@ubuntu-node01:~$ docker container exec -it container-null-net ifconfig
lo        Link encap:Local Loopback
          inet addr:127.0.0.1  Mask:255.0.0.0
          UP LOOPBACK RUNNING  MTU:65536  Metric:1
          RX packets:0 errors:0 dropped:0 overruns:0 frame:0
          TX packets:0 errors:0 dropped:0 overruns:0 carrier:0
          collisions:0 txqueuelen:1000
          RX bytes:0 (0.0 B)  TX bytes:0 (0.0 B)

earl@ubuntu-node01:~$
```

The third network driver with a scope of local is the bridge driver. Bridge networks are the most common type. Any containers attached to the same bridge network are able to communicate with one another. A Docker host can have more than one network created with the bridge driver. However, containers attached to one bridge network are unable to communicate with containers on a different bridge network, even if the networks are on the same Docker host. Note that there are slight feature differences between the built-in bridge network and any user-created bridge networks. It is best practice to create your own bridge networks and utilize them instead of the using the built-in bridge network. Here is an example of running a container using a bridge network:

```
earl@ubuntu-node01:~$ docker container run -d --network bridge --name container-bridge-net alpine tail -f /dev/null
bc57778e9251a6c6a8e169a8b1db54a2eafc6c4c545e4df285401f963cab4c59
earl@ubuntu-node01:~$ docker container exec -it container-bridge-net ifconfig
eth0      Link encap:Ethernet  HWaddr 02:42:AC:11:00:02
          inet addr:172.17.0.2  Bcast:172.17.255.255  Mask:255.255.0.0
          UP BROADCAST RUNNING MULTICAST  MTU:1500  Metric:1
          RX packets:46 errors:0 dropped:0 overruns:0 frame:0
          TX packets:0 errors:0 dropped:0 overruns:0 carrier:0
          collisions:0 txqueuelen:0
          RX bytes:6320 (6.1 KiB)  TX bytes:0 (0.0 B)

lo        Link encap:Local Loopback
          inet addr:127.0.0.1  Mask:255.0.0.0
          UP LOOPBACK RUNNING  MTU:65536  Metric:1
          RX packets:0 errors:0 dropped:0 overruns:0 frame:0
          TX packets:0 errors:0 dropped:0 overruns:0 carrier:0
          collisions:0 txqueuelen:1000
          RX bytes:0 (0.0 B)  TX bytes:0 (0.0 B)

earl@ubuntu-node01:~$
```

In addition to the drivers that create networks with local scope, there are built-in network drivers that create networks with swarm scope. Such networks will span all the hosts in a swarm and allow containers attached to them to communicate in spite of running on different Docker hosts. As you probably have surmised, use of networks that have swarm scope requires Docker swarm mode. In fact, when you initialize a Docker host into swarm mode, a special new network is created for you that has swarm scope. This swarm scope network is named *ingress* and is created using the built-in overlay driver. This network is vital to the load balancing feature of swarm mode that saw used in the *Accessing container applications in a swarm* section of `Chapter 5`, *Docker Swarm*. There's also a new bridge network created in the `swarm init`, named docker_gwbridge. This network is used by swarm to communicate outward, kind of like a default gateway. Here are the default built-in networks found in a new Docker swarm:

```
earl@ubuntu-node01:~$ docker swarm init
Swarm initialized: current node (lqibltiuf61159pkxy2kq2y0l) is now a manager.

To add a worker to this swarm, run the following command:

    docker swarm join --token SWMTKN-1-29r0d3bcip7q8js4odmv1kntygaq9radts0vqv4iatr9avicc

To add a manager to this swarm, run 'docker swarm join-token manager' and follow the ins

earl@ubuntu-node01:~$ docker network ls
NETWORK ID          NAME                DRIVER              SCOPE
32a527a0ec19        bridge              bridge              local
d2529af02e22        docker_gwbridge     bridge              local
7245a5bfc80c        host                host                local
u4kyxxpze6ld        ingress             overlay             swarm
73643f1d3b6a        none                null                local
earl@ubuntu-node01:~$ 
```

Using the overlay driver allows you to create networks that span Docker hosts. These are layer 2 networks. There is a lot of network plumbing that gets laid down behind the scenes when you create an overlay network. Each host in the swarm gets a network sandbox with a network stack. Within that sandbox, a bridge is created and named br0. Then, a VXLAN tunnel endpoint is created and attached to bridge br0. Once all of the swarm hosts have the tunnel endpoint created, a VXLAN tunnel is created that connects all of the endpoints together. This tunnel is actually what we see as the overlay network. When containers are attached to the overlay network, they get an IP address assigned from the overlay's subnet, and all communications between containers on that network are carried out via the overlay. Of course, behind the scenes that communication traffic is passing through the VXLAN endpoints, going across the Docker hosts network, and any routers connecting the host to the networks of the other Docker hosts. But, you never have to worry about all the behind-the-scenes stuff. Just create an overlay network, attach your containers to it, and you're golden.

The next local network driver that we're going to discuss is called MACVLAN. This driver creates networks that allow containers to each have their own IP and MAC addresses, and to be attached to a non-Docker network. What that means is that in addition to the container-to-container communication you get with bridge and overlay networks, with MACVLAN networks you also are able to connect with VLANs, VMs, and other physical servers. Said another way, the MACVLAN driver allows you to get your containers onto existing networks and VLANs. A MACVLAN network has to be created on each Docker host where you will run containers that need to connect to your existing networks. What's more, you will need a different MACVLAN network created for each VLAN you want containers to connect to. While using MACVLAN networks sounds like the way to go, there are two important challenges to using it. First, you have to be very careful about the subnet ranges you assign to the MACVLAN network. Containers will be assigned IPs from your range without any consideration of the IPs in use elsewhere. If you have a DHCP system handing out IPs that overlap with the range you gave to the MACVLAN driver, it can easily cause duplicate IP scenarios. The second challenge is that MACVLAN networks require your network cards to be configured in promiscuous mode. This is usually frowned upon in on-premise networks but is pretty much forbidden in cloud-provider networks such as AWS and Azure, so the MACVLAN driver will have very limited use cases.

There is a lot of information covered in this section on local or built-in network drivers. Don't despair! They are much easier to create and use than this wealth of information seems to indicate. We will go into creating and using info shortly in the *Creating Docker networks* section, but next, let's have a quick discussion about remote (also known as third-party) network drivers.

References

Check out these links for more information:

- Excellent, in-depth Docker article for Docker networking: `https://success.docker.com/article/networking`
- Networking with Overlay Networks: `https://docs.docker.com/network/network-tutorial-overlay/`
- Using MACVLAN networks: `https://docs.docker.com/v17.12/network/macvlan/`

Third-party (remote) network drivers

As mentioned previously in the *What is a Docker network*? section, in addition to the built-in, or local, network drivers provided by Docker, the CNM supports community- and vendor-created network drivers. Some examples of these third-party drivers include Contiv, Weave, Kuryr, and Calico. One of the benefits of using one of these third-party drivers is that they fully support deployment in cloud-hosted environments, such as AWS. In order to use these drivers, they need to be installed in a separate installation step for each of your Docker hosts. Each of the third-party network drivers brings their own set of features to the table. Here is the summary description of these drivers as shared by Docker in the reference architecture document:

Driver	Description
contiv	An open source network plugin led by Cisco Systems to provide infrastructure and security policies for multi-tenant microservices deployments. Contiv also provides integration for non-container workloads and with physical networks, such as ACI. Contiv implements remote network and IPAM drivers.
weave	A network plugin that creates a virtual network that connects Docker containers across multiple hosts or clouds. Weave provides automatic discovery of applications, can operate on partially connected networks, does not require an external cluster store, and is operations friendly.
calico	An open source solution for virtual networking in cloud datacenters. It targets datacenters where most of the workloads (VMs, containers, or bare metal servers) only require IP connectivity. Calico provides this connectivity using standard IP routing. Isolation between workloads — whether according to tenant ownership or any finer grained policy — is achieved via iptables programming on the servers hosting the source and destination workloads.
kuryr	A network plugin developed as part of the OpenStack Kuryr project. It implements the Docker networking (libnetwork) remote driver API by utilizing Neutron, the OpenStack networking service. Kuryr includes an IPAM driver as well.

Although each of these third-party drivers has its own unique installation, setup, and execution methods, the general steps are similar. First, you download the driver, then you handle any configuration setup, and finally you run the driver. These remote drivers typically do not require swarm mode and can be used with or without it. As an example, let's take a deep-dive into using the weave driver. To install the weave network driver, issue the following commands on each Docker host:

```
# Install the weave network driver plug-in
sudo curl -L git.io/weave -o /usr/local/bin/weave
sudo chmod a+x /usr/local/bin/weave
# Disable checking for new versions
export CHECKPOINT_DISABLE=1
# Start up the weave network
weave launch [for 2nd, 3rd, etc. optional hostname or IP of 1st Docker host running weave]
# Set up the environment to use weave
eval $(weave env)
```

The preceding steps need to be completed on each Docker host that will be used to run containers that will communicate with each other over the weave network. The launch command can provide the hostname or IP address of the first Docker host, which was set up and already running the weave network, to peer with it so that their containers can communicate. For example, if you have set up node01 with the weave network when you start up weave on node02, you would use the following command:

```
# Start up weave on the 2nd node
weave launch node01
```

Alternatively, you can connect new (Docker host) peers using the connect command, executing it from the first host configured. To add node02 (after it has weave installed and running), use the following command:

```
# Peer host node02 with the weave network by connecting from node01
weave connect node02
```

You can utilize the weave network driver without enabling swarm mode on your hosts. Once weave has been installed and started, and the peers (other Docker hosts) have been connected, your containers will automatically utilize the weave network and be able to communicate with each other regardless of whether they are on the same Docker host or different ones.

The weave network shows up in your network list just like any of your other networks:

```
earl@ubuntu-node01:~$ docker network ls
NETWORK ID          NAME          DRIVER          SCOPE
5d961eee7220        bridge        bridge          local
7245a5bfc80c        host          host            local
73643f1d3b6a        none          null            local
9c4b9d45835c        weave         weavemesh       local
earl@ubuntu-node01:~$
```

Let's test out our shiny new network. First, make sure that you have installed the weave driver on all the hosts you want to be connected by following the steps described previously. Make sure that you either use the launch command with node01 as a parameter, or from node01 you use the connect command for each of the additional nodes you are configuring. For this example, my lab servers are named ubuntu-node01 and ubuntu-node02. Let's start with node02:

Note the following, on ubuntu-node01:

```
# Install and setup the weave driver
sudo curl -L git.io/weave -o /usr/local/bin/weave
sudo chmod a+x /usr/local/bin/weave
export CHECKPOINT_DISABLE=1
weave launch
eval $(weave env)
```

And, note the following, on ubuntu-node02:

```
# Install and setup the weave driver
sudo curl -L git.io/weave -o /usr/local/bin/weave
sudo chmod a+x /usr/local/bin/weave
export CHECKPOINT_DISABLE=1
weave launch
eval $(weave env)
```

Now, back on ubuntu-node01, note the following:

```
# Bring node02 in as a peer on node01's weave network
weave connect ubuntu-node02
```

```
earl@ubuntu-node01:~$ weave connect ubuntu-node02
earl@ubuntu-node01:~$
```

Now, let's launch a container on each node. Make sure we name them for easy identification, starting with `ubuntu-node01`:

```
# Run a container detached on node01
docker container run -d --name app01 alpine tail -f /dev/null
```

```
earl@ubuntu-node01:~$ docker container run -d --name app01 alpine tail -f /dev/null
Unable to find image 'alpine:latest' locally
latest: Pulling from library/alpine
4fe2ade4980c: Pull complete
Digest: sha256:621c2f39f8133acb8e64023a94dbdf0d5ca81896102b9e57c0dc184cadaf5528
Status: Downloaded newer image for alpine:latest
2fa85c83e545235ef5a82cf4fb5b933328b86ff5f93571f0450f0d7b5aef4b7f
earl@ubuntu-node01:~$ ▊
```

Now, launch a container on `ubuntu-node02`:

```
# Run a container detached on node02
docker container run -d --name app02 alpine tail -f /dev/null
```

```
earl@ubuntu-node02:~$ docker container run -d --name app02 alpine tail -f /dev/null
Unable to find image 'alpine:latest' locally
latest: Pulling from library/alpine
4fe2ade4980c: Pull complete
Digest: sha256:621c2f39f8133acb8e64023a94dbdf0d5ca81896102b9e57c0dc184cadaf5528
Status: Downloaded newer image for alpine:latest
81d238d31f0a4b4174f6db11cf04b5cafe783e750671d1c3fecb423029af6adf
earl@ubuntu-node02:~$ ▊
```

Excellent. Now, we have containers running on both nodes. Let's see whether they can communicate. Since we are on `node02`, we will check there first:

```
# From inside the app02 container running on node02,
# let's ping the app01 container running on node01
docker container exec -it app02 ping -c 4 app01
```

```
earl@ubuntu-node02:~$ docker container exec -it app02 ping -c 4 app01
PING app01 (10.40.0.0): 56 data bytes
64 bytes from 10.40.0.0: seq=0 ttl=64 time=0.739 ms
64 bytes from 10.40.0.0: seq=1 ttl=64 time=0.278 ms
64 bytes from 10.40.0.0: seq=2 ttl=64 time=0.324 ms
64 bytes from 10.40.0.0: seq=3 ttl=64 time=0.291 ms

--- app01 ping statistics ---
4 packets transmitted, 4 packets received, 0% packet loss
round-trip min/avg/max = 0.278/0.408/0.739 ms
earl@ubuntu-node02:~$
```

Yeah! That worked. Let's try going the other way:

```
# Similarly, from inside the app01 container running on node01,
# let's ping the app02 container running on node02
docker container exec -it app01 ping -c 4 app02
```

```
earl@ubuntu-node01:~$ docker container exec -it app01 ping -c 4 app02
PING app02 (10.32.0.1): 56 data bytes
64 bytes from 10.32.0.1: seq=0 ttl=64 time=0.284 ms
64 bytes from 10.32.0.1: seq=1 ttl=64 time=0.287 ms
64 bytes from 10.32.0.1: seq=2 ttl=64 time=0.299 ms
64 bytes from 10.32.0.1: seq=3 ttl=64 time=0.246 ms

--- app02 ping statistics ---
4 packets transmitted, 4 packets received, 0% packet loss
round-trip min/avg/max = 0.246/0.279/0.299 ms
earl@ubuntu-node01:~$
```

Perfect! We have bi-directional communication. Did you notice anything else? We have name resolution for our app containers (we didn't have to ping by IP only). Pretty nice, right?

References

Check out these links for more information:

- Installing and using the weave network driver: https://www.weave.works/docs/net/latest/overview/
- Weaveworks weave github repo: https://github.com/weaveworks/weave

Creating Docker networks

OK, you now know a lot about both the local and the remote network drivers, and you have seen how several of them are created for you when you install Docker and/or initialize swarm mode (or install a remote driver). But, what if you want to create your own networks using some of these drivers? It is really pretty simple. Let's take a look. The built-in help for the `network create` command looks like this:

```
# Docker network create command syntax
# Usage: docker network create [OPTIONS] NETWORK
```

Examining this, we see there are essentially two parts of this command we need to handle, the OPTIONS followed by the NETWORK name to make the network we wish to create. What are our options? Well, there are quite a lot, but let's pick out a few to get you going quickly.

Probably the most important option is the `--driver` option. This is how we tell Docker which of the pluggable network drivers to use when creating this network. As you have seen, the choice of driver determines the network characteristics. The value you supply to the driver option will be like the ones shown in the DRIVER column of the output from the `docker network ls` command. Some of the possible values are bridge, overlay, and macvlan. Remember that you cannot create additional host or null networks as they are limited to one per Docker host. So far, what might this look like? Here is an example of creating a new overlay network, using mostly defaults for options:

```
# Create a new overlay network, with all default options
docker network create -d overlay defaults-over
```

That works just fine. You can run new services and attach them to your new network. But what else might we want to control in our network? Well, how about the IP space? Yep, and Docker provides options for controlling the IP settings for our networks. This is done using the `--subnet`, `--gateway`, and `--ip-range` optional parameters. So, let's take a look at creating a new network using this options. See Chapter 2, *Learning Docker Commands*, for how to install jq if you have not done so already:

```
# Create a new overlay network with specific IP settings
docker network create -d overlay \
--subnet=172.30.0.0/24 \
--ip-range=172.30.0.0/28 \
--gateway=172.30.0.254 \
specifics-over
# Initial validation
docker network inspect specifics-over --format '{{json .IPAM.Config}}' | jq
```

Executing the preceding code in my lab looks like this:

```
earl@ubuntu-node01:~$ docker network create -d overlay \
> --subnet=172.30.0.0/24 \
> --ip-range=172.30.0.0/28 \
> --gateway=172.30.0.254 \
> specifics-over
8hg4r4wflap7pum8jdkk23s6y
earl@ubuntu-node01:~$ docker network inspect specifics-over --format '{{json .IPAM.Config}}' | jq
[
  {
    "Subnet": "172.30.0.0/24",
    "IPRange": "172.30.0.0/28",
    "Gateway": "172.30.0.254"
  }
]
earl@ubuntu-node01:~$ docker service create --quiet --replicas 3 --name tester1 \
> --network specifics-over alpine tail -f /dev/null
6yoki3vrd88u2l0l86uzy2bl0
earl@ubuntu-node01:~$ docker container ls
CONTAINER ID    IMAGE           COMMAND              CREATED         STATUS         PORTS
7536f21ab187    alpine:latest   "tail -f /dev/null"  19 seconds ago  Up 17 seconds
hls3lns
earl@ubuntu-node01:~$ docker container inspect 7536 --format '{{json .NetworkSettings.Networks}}' | jq
{
  "specifics-over": {
    "IPAMConfig": {
      "IPv4Address": "172.30.0.7"
    },
    "Links": null,
    "Aliases": [
      "7536f21ab187"
    ],
    "NetworkID": "8hg4r4wflap7pum8jdkk23s6y",
    "EndpointID": "fd9999d57d264dd068404c33e8be3f1c6a0c9987609f9244b9644e0ae4ee365f",
    "Gateway": "",
    "IPAddress": "172.30.0.7",
    "IPPrefixLen": 24,
```

Looking over this example, we see that we created a new overlay network using specific IP parameters for the subnet, the IP range, and the gateway. Then, we validated that the network was created with the requested options. Next, we created a service using our new network. Then, we found the container ID for a container belonging to the service and used it to inspect the network settings for the container. We can see that the container was run using an IP address (in this case, `172.30.0.7`) from the IP range we configured our network with. Looks like we made it!

As mentioned, there are many other options available when creating Docker networks, and I will leave it as an exercise for you to discover them with the `docker network create --help` command, and to try some of them out to see what they do.

References

You can find the documentation for the `network create` command at `https://docs.docker.com/engine/reference/commandline/network_create/`.

Free networking features

There are two networking features or services that you get for free with your Docker swarm networks. The first is Service Discovery, and the second is load balancing. When you create Docker services, you get these features automatically. We experienced these features in this chapter and in `Chapter 5`, *Docker Swarm*, but didn't really refer to them by name. So, let's call them out here.

First up is Service Discovery. When you create a service, it gets a unique name. That name gets registered with the swarm DNS. And, every service uses the swarm DNS for name resolution. Here is an example for you. We are going to leverage the `specifics-over` overlay network we created earlier in the creating Docker networks section. We'll create two services (`tester1` and `tester2`) attached to that network, then we will connect to a container in the `tester1` services and ping the `tester2` service by name. Check it out:

```
# Create service tester1
docker service create --detach --replicas 3 --name tester1 \
  --network specifics-over alpine tail -f /dev/null
# Create service tester2
docker service create --detach --replicas 3 --name tester2 \
  --network specifics-over alpine tail -f /dev/null
# From a container in the tester1 service ping the tester2 service by name
docker container exec -it tester1.3.5hj309poppj8jo272ks9n4k6a ping -c 3
tester2
```

Here is what the preceding commands look like when executed:

```
earl@ubuntu-node01:~$ docker service create --detach --replicas 3 --name tester1 \
>    --network specifics-over alpine tail -f /dev/null
vtsv7qrveiqos9guvqdrfgjgp
earl@ubuntu-node01:~$ docker service create --detach --replicas 3 --name tester2 \
>    --network specifics-over alpine tail -f /dev/null
trof7inl4ey4xc5ohzw9yf2n3
earl@ubuntu-node01:~$ docker container exec -it tester1.3.5hj309poppj8jo272ks9n4k6a ping -c 3 tester2
PING tester2 (172.30.0.8): 56 data bytes
64 bytes from 172.30.0.8: seq=0 ttl=64 time=0.056 ms
64 bytes from 172.30.0.8: seq=1 ttl=64 time=0.068 ms
64 bytes from 172.30.0.8: seq=2 ttl=64 time=0.063 ms

--- tester2 ping statistics ---
3 packets transmitted, 3 packets received, 0% packet loss
round-trip min/avg/max = 0.056/0.062/0.068 ms
earl@ubuntu-node01:~$
```

Note that I typed the first part of the service name (tester1) and used command-line completion by hitting *Tab* to fill in the container name for the exec command. But, as you can see, I was able to reference the tester2 service by name from within a tester1 container.

For free!

The second free feature we get is Load balancing. This powerful feature is pretty easy to understand. It allows traffic intended for a service to be sent to any host in a swarm regardless of whether that host is running a replica of the service.

Imagine a scenario where you have a six-node swarm cluster, and a service that has only one replica deployed. You can send traffic to that service via any host in the swarm and know that it will arrive at the service's one container no matter which host the container is actually running on. In fact, you can direct traffic to all hosts in the swarm using a load balancer, say in a round-robin model, and each time traffic is sent to the load balancer, that traffic will get delivered to the app container without fail.

Pretty handy, right? Again, for free!

References

Want to have a go at service discovery? Then check out https://training.play-with-docker.com/swarm-service-discovery/.

You can read about swarm service load balancing at https://docs.docker.com/engine/swarm/key-concepts/#load-balancing.

Which Docker network driver should I use?

The short answer to that question is the right one for the job. That means there is no single network driver that is the right fit for every situation. If you're doing work on your laptop, running with swarm inactive, and you just need your containers to be able to communicate with each other, the simple bridge mode driver is ideal.

If you have multiple nodes and just need container-to-container traffic, the overlay driver is the right one to use. This one works well in AWS, if you are within the container-to-container realm. If you need container-to-VM or container-to-physical-server communication (and can tolerate promiscuous mode), the MACVLAN driver is the way to go. Or, if you have a more complex requirement, one of the many remote drivers might be just what the doctor ordered.

I've found that for most multi-host scenarios, the overlay driver will get the job done, so I would recommend that you enable swarm mode, and give the overlay driver a try before you ramp up to any of the other multi-host options.

Summary

How do you feel about Docker networking now? Docker has taken a complex technology, networking, and made it easy to understand and use. Most of the crazy, difficult setup stuff is literally handled with a single `swarm init` command. Let's review: you learned about the network design that Docker created, called the container network model, or CNM. Then, you learned how the libnetwork project turned that model into a pluggable architecture. After that, you found out that Docker created a powerful set of drivers to plug into the libnetwork architecture to enable a variety of network options for most of your container communication needs. Since the architecture is so pluggable, others have created even more network drivers that solve any edge cases that the Docker drivers don't handle. Docker networking has really come into its own.

I hope you are ready for more, because in Chapter 7, *Docker Stacks*, we are going to dive into Docker stacks. This is where all of the information you have learned so far really comes together into a symphony of brilliance. Take a deep breath and turn the page!

7
Docker Stacks

In this chapter, we will bring together all that we've learned from the first six chapters and use it to define, deploy, and manage multi-container applications. We will achieve this via the use of Docker stacks. We are going to learn how to use Docker stacks and the YAML files required to define multi-container applications. And we will leverage what we learned about Docker services, Docker volumes, Docker swarm, and Docker networking to create full-featured multi-service Docker-based applications.

> *The largest cargo ship is 400 meters long and can carry between 15,000 and 18,000 shipping containers!*

In this chapter, we will cover the following topics:

- Using Docker stacks
- Deploying a multi-service Docker application
- Creating and using compose (stack) YAML files
- Scaling a deployed multi-service Docker application

Technical requirements

You will be pulling Docker images from Docker's public repo, and installing network drivers from Weave, so basic internet access is required to execute the examples within this chapter. Also, we will be using the jq software package, so if you haven't installed it yet, please see the instructions on how to do so; they can be found in the *Container inspect command* section of Chapter 2, *Learning Docker Commands*.

The code files of this chapter can be found on GitHub:
https://github.com/PacktPublishing/Docker-Quick-Start-Guide/tree/master/Chapter07

Check out the following video to see the code in action:
http://bit.ly/2E2qc9U

Understanding the use of Docker stacks

So far, we have mostly been looking at running a Docker container from a single Docker image, simplifying the Docker model to imagine a world where every application only required a single service, and thus a single Docker image, to run. However, as you know, that is a pretty unrealistic model. Real-world applications are composed of multiple services, and those services are deployed using multiple Docker images. To run all of the necessary containers, and maintain them at the desired number of replicas, handling planned and unplanned downtimes, scaling requirements and all of the other service management needs is a really daunting and complex task. In the recent past, this scenario was handled using a tool called Docker Compose. Docker Compose (as you learned in Chapter 1, *Setting up a Docker Development Environment*) is an additional tool that you can install in your Docker environment, which we did to complete our workstation's environment. While much of the functionality of Docker Compose is similar to what you find in Docker stacks, we will be focusing on Docker stacks in this chapter. We are doing this because Docker Compose is used to manage containers, and the Docker world has evolved toward the commodity unit being services instead of containers. Docker stacks manages services, and so I see Docker stacks as the evolution of Docker Compose (which was the evolution of a project named Fig). The reason we did not install Docker stacks in Chapter 1, *Setting up a Docker Development Environment*, is that Stacks is already included as part of a standard Docker installation.

OK, so Docker stacks is the new and improved Docker Compose, and it is included in our installation. I bet you're thinking, Great. But what does that mean? What is the use case of Docker stacks? Great question! Docker stacks is *the* way to leverage all of the functionality that we have learned about in the earlier chapters, such as the Docker commands, Docker images, Docker services, Docker volumes, Docker swarm, and Docker networks, wrapping it all up in an easy-to-use, easy-to-understand, declarative document file that will instantiate and maintain a complex, multi-image application on our behalf.

Most of your work, which is still the easy part, will be in creating the compose file that will be used in the Docker stack commands. All of the really hard work will be done by Docker when it creates, starts, and manages all of the services required for your multi-service (multi-container) applications. All of this is handled by a single command on your part. Just like image, the container and swarm stacks are another Docker management group. Let's take a look at the stack management commands:

```
earl@ubuntu-node01:~$ docker stack --help

Usage:  docker stack [OPTIONS] COMMAND

Manage Docker stacks

Options:
      --orchestrator string   Orchestrator to use (swarm|kubernetes|all)

Commands:
  deploy     Deploy a new stack or update an existing stack
  ls         List stacks
  ps         List the tasks in the stack
  rm         Remove one or more stacks
  services   List the services in the stack

Run 'docker stack COMMAND --help' for more information on a command.
earl@ubuntu-node01:~$
```

So, what do we have here? For all the power that this management group represents, it has a pretty simple set of commands. The main command is the deploy command. It is the powerhouse! With this command (and a compose file), you will stand up your application, pulling any images that are not local to your environment, running the images, creating volumes as needed, creating networks as needed, deploying the defined number of replicas for each image, spreading them across your swarm for HA and load-balancing purposes, and more. This command is kind of like the one ring in *The Lord of the Rings*. In addition to deploying your application, you will use this same command to update running applications, when you need to do things such as scale your application.

The next command in the management group is the list stacks command. As the name implies, the ls command allows you to get a list of all the stacks currently deployed to your swarm. When you need more detailed information about a particular stack that is running in your swarm, you will use the ps command to list all of the tasks of a particular stack. When it comes time to end of life a deployed stack, you will use the mighty rm command. And finally, rounding out the management commands, we have the services command, which allows us to get a list of the services that are part of the stack. There is one more important part of the stack puzzle, that being the --orchestrator option. With this option, we can instruct Docker to use either Docker swarm or Kubernetes for the stack orchestration. Of course, to use Kubernetes, it must be installed, and to use swarm—which is the default if the option is not specified—swarm mode must be enabled.

In the rest of this chapter, we are going to take a deep dive into Docker stacks using a sample application. Docker provides several such samples, but the one we are going to examine is the voting application sample. I will provide a link to the Docker repo for the app, as well as a link to a fork of the project in my space in the event that the Docker app changes drastically or the project goes away. Let's take a look at the stack file for the example voting application.

References

Check out the following links for more information:

- Docker Compose Overview: `https://docs.docker.com/compose/overview/`
- Docker stack command reference: `https://docs.docker.com/engine/reference/commandline/stack/`
- Docker samples: `https://github.com/dockersamples`
- Docker voting app example: `https://github.com/dockersamples/example-voting-app`
- My fork of the voting app: `https://github.com/EarlWaud/example-voting-app`

How to create and use a compose YAML files for Stacks

The stack file is a YAML file, and is basically the same thing as a Docker Compose file. Both are YAML files that define a Docker base application. Technically, a stack file is a compose file that requires a specific version (or above) of the compose specification. Only the version 3.0 specification and above are supported by Docker stacks. If you have an existing project that uses Docker compose YAML files, and those files are using the version 2 or older specification, then you will need to update the YAML files to the version 3 spec to be able to use them with Docker stacks. It is worth noting that the same YAML file can be used with either Docker stacks or Docker compose (provided it is written using the version 3 specification or higher). However, there are some instructions that will be ignored by one or the other tools. For example, the build instruction is ignored by Docker stacks. That is because one of the most significant differences between stacks and compose is that all utilized Docker images must be pre-created for use with stacks, whereas Docker images can be created as part of the process of standing up a compose-based application. Another significant difference is the stack file is able to define Docker services as part of the application.

Now would be a good time to clone the voting app project and the visualizer image repos:

```
# Clone the sample voting application and the visualizer repos
git clone https://github.com/EarlWaud/example-voting-app.git
git clone https://github.com/EarlWaud/docker-swarm-visualizer.git
```

Strictly speaking, you don't need to clone these two repos because all you really need is the stack compose file from the voting app. This is because all of the images are already created and publicly available to pull from hub.docker.com, and when you deploy the stack, the images will be pulled for you as part of the deployment. So, here is the command to obtain just the stack YAML file:

```
# Use curl to get the stack YAML file
curl -o docker-stack.yml\
https://raw.githubusercontent.com/earlwaud/example-voting-app/master/docker
-stack.yml
```

Of course, if you want to customize the app in any way, having the project local allows you to build your own versions of the Docker images and then deploy your custom version of the app using your custom images.

Once you have the project (or at least the `docker-stack.yml` file) on your system, you can begin to play around with the Docker stack commands. So now, let's go ahead and kick things off by using the `docker-stack.yml` file to deploy our application. You will need to have your Docker nodes set up and have swarm mode enabled for this to work, so if you haven't done so already, set up your swarm as described in Chapter 5, *Docker Swarm*. Then, use the following command to deploy your example voting application:

```
# Deploy the example voting application
# using the downloaded stack YAML file
docker stack deploy -c docker-stack.yml voteapp
```

Here is what this might look like:

```
earl@ubuntu-node01:~$ curl -o docker-stack.yml \
>     https://raw.githubusercontent.com/earlwaud/example-voting-app/master/docker-stack.yml
 % Total    % Received % Xferd  Average Speed   Time    Time     Time  Current
                                 Dload  Upload   Total   Spent    Left  Speed
100  1692  100  1692    0     0    936      0  0:00:01  0:00:01 --:--:--   935
earl@ubuntu-node01:~$ docker stack deploy -c docker-stack.yml voteapp
Creating network voteapp_backend
Creating network voteapp_frontend
Creating network voteapp_default
Creating service voteapp_visualizer
Creating service voteapp_redis
Creating service voteapp_db
Creating service voteapp_vote
Creating service voteapp_result
Creating service voteapp_worker
earl@ubuntu-node01:~$ █
```

Let me quickly explaining this command: we are using the `deploy` command with the `docker-stack.yml` compose file, and naming our stack `voteapp`. This command will handle all of the configuration, deployment, and management for our new application. It will take some time to get everything up and running as defined in the `docker-stack.yml` file, so while that is happening, let's start diving into our stack compose file.

By now, you know we are using the `docker-stack.yml` file. So, as we explain the various parts of the stack compose file, you can bring that file up in your favorite editor, and follow along. Here we go!

The first thing we are going to look at is the top-level keys. In this case, they are as follows:

- version
- services
- networks
- volumes

As mentioned previously, the version must be at least 3 to work with Docker stacks. Looking at line 1 (the version key is always on line 1) in the `docker-stack.yml` file, we see the following:

```
 1  version: "3"
 2  services: ▦
83
84  networks:
85    frontend:
86    backend:
87
88  volumes:
89    db-data:|
```

Perfect! We have a compose file that is at the version 3 specification. Skipping over the (collapsed) services key section for a minute, let's take a look at the networks key and then the volumes key. In the networks key section, we are instructing Docker to create two networks, one named frontend, and one named backend. Actually, in our case, the networks will have the names `voteapp_frontend` and `voteapp_backend`. This is because we named our stack `voteapp`, and Docker will prepend the name of the stack to the various components it deploys as part of the stack. Simply by including the names for our desired networks within the networks key of our stack file, Docker will create our networks when we deploy our stack. We can provide specific details for each network (as we learned in `Chapter 6`, *Docker Networking*), but if we don't provide any, then certain default values will be used. It's probably been long enough for our stack to deploy our networks, so let's use the network list command and take a look at what networks we have now:

```
earl@ubuntu-node01:~$ docker network ls
NETWORK ID          NAME                DRIVER              SCOPE
5f2edb01b2f8        bridge              bridge              local
ace05d900871        docker_gwbridge     bridge              local
7245a5bfc80c        host                host                local
788oyjwf0pcv        ingress             overlay             swarm
73643f1d3b6a        none                null                local
m6sh1d97dhhd        voteapp_backend     overlay             swarm
qk06igkd36z6        voteapp_default     overlay             swarm
fd8e4q19kz3l        voteapp_frontend    overlay             swarm
```

There they are: `voteapp_frontend` and `voteapp_backend`. You might be wondering what the `voteapp_default` network is. When you deploy a stack, you will always get a default swarm network and all containers are attached to it if they don't have any other network connection defined for them in the stack compose file. This is very cool, right?! You didn't have to do any docker network create commands, and your desired networks are created and ready to use in your application.

The volumes key section does pretty much the same thing as the networks key section, except it does it for volumes. You get your defined volumes created automatically when you deploy the stack. The volumes are created with default settings if no additional configuration is provided in the stack file. In our example, we are asking Docker to create a volume named `db-data`. As you may have guessed, the volume created actually has the name of `voteapp_db-data` because Docker prepended the name of our stack to the volume name. In our case, it looks like this:

```
earl@ubuntu-node01:~$ docker volume ls
DRIVER                  VOLUME NAME
local                   voteapp_db-data
earl@ubuntu-node01:~$
```

So, deploying our stack created our desired networks and our desired volume. All with the easy-to-create, and easy-to-read-and-understand content in our stack compose file. OK, so we now have a good grasp of three of the four top-level key sections in our stack compose file. Now, let's return to the services key section. If we expand this key section, we will see definitions for each of the services we wish to deploy as part of the application. In the case of the `docker-stack.yml` file, we have six services defined. These are redis, db, vote, result, worker, and visualizer. In the stack compose file, they look like this:

```
 2▾ services:
 3▸   redis: ▪
16▸   db: ▪
25▸   vote: ▪
39▸   result: ▪
54▸   worker: ▪
70▸   visualizer: ▪
```

Let's expand the first one, redis, and take a closer look at what is defined as the redis service for our application:

```
 2  services:
 3    redis:
 4      image: redis:alpine
 5      ports:
 6        - "6379"
 7      networks:
 8        - frontend
 9      deploy:
10        replicas: 1
11        update_config:
12          parallelism: 2
13          delay: 10s
14        restart_policy:
15          condition: on-failure
```

If you recall the discussion of Docker services from `Chapter 5`, *Docker Swarm*, many of the keys shown here should seem familiar to you. Let's examine the keys in the redis service now. First up, we have the `image` key. The image key is required for the service definition. This key is telling docker that the Docker image to pull and run for this service is `redis:alpine`. As you should understand now, this means that we are using the official redis image from hub.docker.com, requesting the version tagged as `alpine`. The next key, `ports`, is defining what port the images will be exposing from the container, and from the hosts. In this case, the port on the host that is to be mapped to the container's exposed port (`6379`) is left to Docker to assign. You can find the port assigned using the `docker container ls` command. In my case, the redis service is mapping port `30000` on the host to port `6379` on the container. The next key used is `networks`. We already have seen that deploying the stack will create our networks for us. This directive is telling Docker which networks that the redis replica containers should be connected to; in this case it is the `frontend` network. If we inspect a redis replica container, examining the networks section, we will see this to be accurate. You can have a look at your deployment with a command such as this (note that the container name will be slightly different on your system):

```
# Inspect a redis replica container looking at the networks
docker container inspect voteapp_redis.1.nwy14um7ik0t7ul0j5t3aztu5 \
    --format '{{json .NetworkSettings.Networks}}' | jq
```

In our example, you should see that the container is attached to two networks: the ingress network and our `voteapp_frontend` network.

The next key in our redis service definition is the deploy key. This is a key category that was added to the compose file specification with version 3. It is what defines the specifics for running the containers based on the image in this service: in this case, the redis image. It is essentially the orchestration instructions. The `replicas` tag tells docker how many copies or containers should be running when the application is fully deployed. In our example, we are stating that we only need one instance of the redis container running for our application. The `update_config` key provides two sub keys, `parallelism` and `delay`, that tell Docker how many container `replicas` should be started in parallel, and how much time to wait between starting each `parallel` set of container `replicas`. Of course, with one replica, the parallelism and delay details have little use. If the value for `replicas` were something greater, such as `10`, our update_config keys would result in two replicas starting at a time, with a wait of 10 seconds between starts. The final deploy key is `restart_policy`, and this defines the conditions that a new replica will be created in a deployed stack. In this case, if a redis container fails, a new redis container will be started to take its place. Let's take a look at the next service in our application, the db service:

```
 2  services:
 3    redis: ▥
16    db:
17      image: postgres:9.4
18      volumes:
19        - db-data:/var/lib/postgresql/data
20      networks:
21        - backend
22      deploy:
23        placement:
24          constraints: [node.role == manager]
```

The db service will have several keys in common with the redis service, but with different values. First, we have the image key. This time we are indicating that we want the official postgres image with the tag for version 9.4. Our next key is the volumes key. We are indicating that we are using the volume named db-data, and that in the DB container the volume should be mounted at `/var/lib/postgresql/data`. Let's take a look at the volume information in our environment:

```
earl@ubuntu-node01:~$ docker volume inspect voteapp_db-data
[
    {
        "CreatedAt": "2018-10-23T19:34:33-07:00",
        "Driver": "local",
        "Labels": {
            "com.docker.stack.namespace": "voteapp"
        },
        "Mountpoint": "/var/lib/docker/volumes/voteapp_db-data/_data",
        "Name": "voteapp_db-data",
        "Options": null,
        "Scope": "local"
    }
]
```

Using the volume inspect command, we get the volume mount point and then compare the contents of the folder within the container to the contents of the mount point on the host:

```
earl@ubuntu-node01:~$ docker container exec -it voteapp_db.1.nm780s46rrvofyp0um6gu7r2h /bin/bash
root@251d07188d86:/# ls /var/lib/postgresql/data
base      pg_dynshmem   pg_logical   pg_replslot   pg_stat      pg_tblspc    pg_xlog                postmaster.opts
global    pg_hba.conf   pg_multixact pg_serial     pg_stat_tmp  pg_twophase  postgresql.auto.conf   postmaster.pid
pg_clog   pg_ident.conf pg_notify    pg_snapshots  pg_subtrans  PG_VERSION   postgresql.conf
root@251d07188d86:/# exit
exit
earl@ubuntu-node01:~$ sudo ls /var/lib/docker/volumes/voteapp_db-data/_data
[sudo] password for earl:
base      pg_dynshmem   pg_logical   pg_replslot   pg_stat      pg_tblspc    pg_xlog                postmaster.opts
global    pg_hba.conf   pg_multixact pg_serial     pg_stat_tmp  pg_twophase  postgresql.auto.conf   postmaster.pid
pg_clog   pg_ident.conf pg_notify    pg_snapshots  pg_subtrans  PG_VERSION   postgresql.conf
earl@ubuntu-node01:~$
```

Voila! As expected, they match. This is not as straightforward on a Mac. See Chapter 4, *Docker Volumes,* on Docker volumes for details on how to handle this on OS X. The next key is the networks key, and here we are directing Docker to attach the backend network to our db container. Next up is the deploy key. Here, we see a new sub-key, called placement. This is a directive to tell Docker that we only want db containers to run on manager nodes, that is, on nodes that have the role of manager.

You may have noticed that there are some sub-keys of the deploy key that are present in the redis service, but are absent in our db service—most notably, the `replicas` key. By default, if you do not specify the number of replicas to maintain, Docker will default to having one replica. All in all, the description of the db service configuration is pretty much the same as the redis service. You will see this similarity between the configuration of all the services. This is because Docker has made it very easy to define the desired state of our services, and by correlation, our applications. To validate this, let's take a look at the next service in the stack compose file, the `vote` service:

```
25    vote:
26      image: dockersamples/examplevotingapp_vote:before
27      ports:
28        - 5000:80
29      networks:
30        - frontend
31      depends_on:
32        - redis
33      deploy:
34        replicas: 2
35        update_config:
36          parallelism: 2
37        restart_policy:
38          condition: on-failure
```

You should be starting to get familiar with these keys and their values. Here in the vote service we see that the image defined is not one of the official container images, but instead is in a public repo named `dockersamples`. Within that repo, we are using the image named `examplevotingapp_vote`, with a version tag of `before`. Our ports key is telling Docker, and us, that we want to open port `5000` on the swarm hosts and have traffic on that port mapped to port 80 in the running vote service containers. As it turns out, the vote service is the `face` of our application and we will access it via port `5000`. Since it is a service, we can access it by going to port `5000` on *any* of the hosts in the swarm, even when a particular host is not running one of the replicas.

Looking at the next key, we see that we are attaching the `frontend` network to our vote service containers. Nothing new there, however, as our next key is one we have not seen before: the `depends_on` key. This key is telling Docker that our vote service requires the redis service to function. What this means to our `deploy` command is that the service or services that are depended on need to be started before starting this service. Specifically, the redis service needs to be started before the vote service. One key distinction here is that I said started. This does not mean that the depended-upon service has to be running before starting this service; the depended-on service just has to be started before it. Again, specifically, the redis service does not have to be at the state of running before starting the vote service, it just has to be started before the vote service is started. There is nothing we haven't seen yet in the deploy key in for the vote service, with the only difference being that we are asking for two replicas for the vote service. Are you beginning to understand the simplicity and the power of the service definition in the stack compose file?

The next service defined in our stack compose file is for the result service. However, since there are no keys present in that service definition that we haven't seen in the previous services, I will skip the discussion on the result service, and move on to the worker service where we'll see some new stuff. Here is the worker service definition:

```
54    worker:
55      image: dockersamples/examplevotingapp_worker
56      networks:
57        - frontend
58        - backend
59      deploy:
60        mode: replicated
61        replicas: 1
62        labels: [APP=VOTING]
63        restart_policy:
64          condition: on-failure
65          delay: 10s
66          max_attempts: 3
67          window: 120s
68        placement:
69          constraints: [node.role == manager]
```

You know about the image key and what it means. You know about the networks key and what it means too. You know about the deploy key, but we have some new sub-keys here so let's talk about them, starting with the `mode` key. You may recall from our discussion of services in Chapter 5, *Docker Swarm*, that there is a `--mode` parameter that can have one of two values: `global` or `replicated`. This key is exactly the same as the parameter we saw in Chapter 5, *Docker Swarm*. The default value is replicated, and so if you do not specify the mode key, you will get the replicated behavior, which is to have exactly the number of replicas that are defined (or one replica if no number of replicas is specified). Using the other value option of global will ignore the replicas key and deploy exactly one container to every host in the swarm.

The next key that we have not seen before in this stack compose file is the `labels` key. The location of this key is significant as it can appear as its own upper-level key, or as a sub-key to the deploy key. What is the distinction? When you use the `labels` key as a sub-key to the deploy key, the label will be set only on the service. When you use the `labels` key as its own upper-level key, the label will be added to each replica, or container, deployed as part of the service. In our example, the `APP=VOTING` label will be applied to the service because the `labels` key is a sub-key to the deploy key. Again, let's see this in our environment:

```
# Inspect the worker service to see its labels
docker service inspect voteapp_worker \
 --format '{{json .Spec.Labels}}' | jq
```

Here is what that looks like on my system:

```
earl@ubuntu-node01:~$ docker service inspect voteapp_worker --format '{{json .Spec.Labels}}' | jq
{
  "APP": "VOTING",
  "com.docker.stack.image": "dockersamples/examplevotingapp_worker",
  "com.docker.stack.namespace": "voteapp"
}
earl@ubuntu-node01:~$
```

Executing an inspect command on a worker container to view the labels on it will show that the `APP=VOTING` label does not appear. If you want to confirm this on your system, the command will look like this (with a different container name):

```
# Inspect the labels on a worker container
docker container inspect voteapp_worker.1.rotx91qw12d6x8643z6iqhuoj \
    -f '{{json .Config.Labels}}' | jq
```

Again, here is what it looks like on my system:

```
earl@ubuntu-node01:~$ docker container inspect voteapp_worker.1.rotx91qw12d6x8643z6iqhuoj -f '{{json .Config.Labels}}' | jq
{
  "com.docker.stack.namespace": "voteapp",
  "com.docker.swarm.node.id": "cj8ncc3wxz3uxjcgqmj8aectg",
  "com.docker.swarm.service.id": "087zvvotv0jxq8mhwr7aig7hi",
  "com.docker.swarm.service.name": "voteapp_worker",
  "com.docker.swarm.task": "",
  "com.docker.swarm.task.id": "rotx91qw12d6x8643z6iqhuoj",
  "com.docker.swarm.task.name": "voteapp_worker.1.rotx91qw12d6x8643z6iqhuoj"
}
earl@ubuntu-node01:~$
```

Two new sub-keys for the restart_policy key are the `max_attempts` and `window` keys. You can probably guess their purpose; the `max_attempts` key tells Docker to keep trying to start the worker containers if they fail to start, up to three times before giving up. The `window` key tells Docker how long to wait before retrying to start a worker container if it failed to start previously. Pretty straightforward, right? Again, these definitions are easy to set up, easy to understand, and extremely powerful for orchestrating the services of our application.

Alright. We have one more service definition to review for new stuff, that being the visualizer service. Here is what it looks like in our stack compose file:

```
70   visualizer:
71     image: dockersamples/visualizer:stable
72     ports:
73       - "8080:8080"
74     stop_grace_period: 1m30s
75     volumes:
76       - "/var/run/docker.sock:/var/run/docker.sock"
77     deploy:
78       placement:
79         constraints: [node.role == manager]
```

The only truly new key is the `stop_grace_period` key. This key tells Docker how long to wait after it tells a container to stop before it will forcefully stop the container. The default time period, if the `stop_grace_period` key is not used, is 10 seconds. When you need to update a stack, essentially do a re-stack, the containers of a service will be told to shut down gracefully. Docker will wait for the amount of time specified in the `stop_grace_period` key, or for 10 seconds if the key is not provided. If the container shuts down during that time, the container will be removed, and a new container will be started in its place. If the container does not shut down during that window of time, it will be stopped by force, killing it, then removing it, then starting a new container to take its place. The significance of this key is that it allows the necessary time for containers that are running processes that take longer to stop gracefully to actually stop gracefully.

The last aspect of this service that I want to point out and that is regarding the kind of strange volume listed. This is not a typical volume and has no entry in the volumes key definitions. The `/var/run/docker.sock:/var/run/docker.sock` volume is a way to access the Unix socket that the host's Docker daemon is listening on. In this case, it's allowing the container to communicate with its host. The visualizer container is gathering information about what containers are running on what hosts and is able to present that data in a graphical way. You will notice that it maps the 8080 host port to the 8080 container port, so we can have a look at what data it shares by browsing to port 8080 on any of our swarm nodes. Here is what it looks like on my (current) three-node swarm:

The rest of the stack commands

Now, let's take a quick look at our other stack-related commands through the lens of the swarm where we deployed our `voteapp` stack. First up, we have the list stacks command: `docker stack ls`. Giving that a try looks like this:

```
# List the stacks deployed in a swarm
docker stack ls
```

Here is what it looks like in the example environment:

```
earl@ubuntu-node01:~$ docker stack ls
NAME              SERVICES         ORCHESTRATOR
voteapp           6                Swarm
earl@ubuntu-node01:~$
```

This is showing that we have one stack named voteapp currently deployed, and that it is composed of six services and is using swarm mode for its orchestration. Knowing the name of a deploy stack allows us to gather more information about it using the other stack commands. Next up is the list stack tasks command. Let's give this command a try in our example environment:

```
# List the tasks for our voteapp stack filtered by desried state
docker stack ps voteapp --filter desired-state=running
```

Here are the results in my environment right now; yours should look very similar:

```
earl@ubuntu-node01:~$ docker stack ps voteapp --filter desired-state=running
ID             NAME                  IMAGE                                             NODE           DESIRED STATE
o5r9lu68nu7o   voteapp_worker.1      dockersamples/examplevotingapp_worker:latest      ubuntu-node01  Running
qs5ed55ptv2i   voteapp_result.1      dockersamples/examplevotingapp_result:before      ubuntu-node03  Running
yaqvbg1k8srp   voteapp_redis.1       redis:alpine                                      ubuntu-node02  Running
w2or9cuh4c4l   voteapp_vote.1        dockersamples/examplevotingapp_vote:before        ubuntu-node01  Running
nm780s46rrvo   voteapp_db.1          postgres:9.4                                      ubuntu-node01  Running
mg8lhaobmzrk   voteapp_visualizer.1  dockersamples/visualizer:stable                   ubuntu-node01  Running
ef88w1d6345e   voteapp_vote.2        dockersamples/examplevotingapp_vote:before        ubuntu-node02  Running
earl@ubuntu-node01:~$
```

Now, we will have a look at the stack services command. This command will give us a nice summary of the services that are deployed as part of our stack application. The command looks like this:

```
# Look at the services associated with a deployed stack
docker stack services voteapp
```

This is what we see in the example environment:

```
earl@ubuntu-node01:~$ docker stack services voteapp
ID              NAME                MODE          REPLICAS   IMAGE                                                PORTS
087zvvotv0jx    voteapp_worker      replicated    1/1        dockersamples/examplevotingapp_worker:latest
27rsidqpykrg    voteapp_visualizer  replicated    1/1        dockersamples/visualizer:stable                      *:8080->8080/tcp
evolo0kef52c    voteapp_db          replicated    1/1        postgres:9.4
kv0iyxct7u9c    voteapp_redis       replicated    1/1        redis:alpine                                         *:30000->6379/tcp
o35d6qoxt7gq    voteapp_vote        replicated    2/2        dockersamples/examplevotingapp_vote:before           *:5000->80/tcp
vfx6qotx6lbz    voteapp_result      replicated    1/1        dockersamples/examplevotingapp_result:before         *:5001->80/tcp
earl@ubuntu-node01:~$ 
```

This command provides some very useful information. We can quickly see the names of our services, the number of replicas desired, and the actual number of replicas for each service. We can see the image used to deploy each service, and we can see the port mapping used for each service. Here, we can see the visualizer service is using port 8080, as we mentioned earlier. We can also see that our vote service is exposed on port 5000 of our swarm hosts. Let's have a look at what we are presenting in our voteapp by browsing to port 5000 (on any node in the swarm) now:

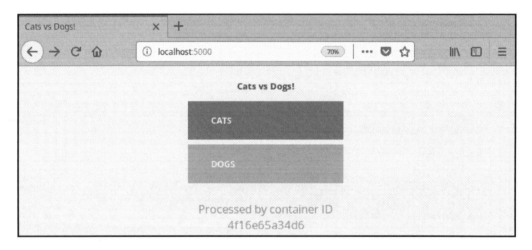

Are you a dog person or a cat person? You can express yourself by voting in your own voteapp! Cast your vote and then use the data in the stack service command to see the results of the vote by browsing to port 5001:

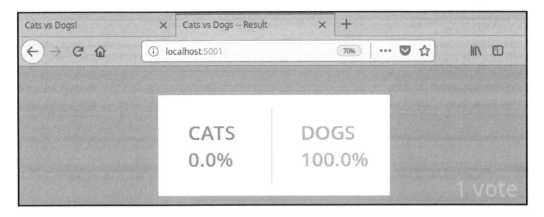

Yes, I am a dog person. There is one final stack command: the remove command. We can quickly and easily take down an application deployed with the stack deploy command by issuing the `rm` command. Here is what that looks like:

```
# Remove a deploy stack using the rm command
docker stack rm voteapp
```

Now you see it, now you don't:

```
earl@ubuntu-node01:~$ docker stack ls
NAME                    SERVICES            ORCHESTRATOR
voteapp                 6                   Swarm
earl@ubuntu-node01:~$ docker stack rm voteapp
Removing service voteapp_db
Removing service voteapp_redis
Removing service voteapp_result
Removing service voteapp_visualizer
Removing service voteapp_vote
Removing service voteapp_worker
Removing network voteapp_frontend
Removing network voteapp_backend
Removing network voteapp_default
earl@ubuntu-node01:~$ docker stack ls
NAME                    SERVICES            ORCHESTRATOR
earl@ubuntu-node01:~$ 
```

You should notice that there was none of the *are you sure?* hand-holding, so be very sure and very careful before pressing *Enter* on this command. Let's close out the discussion on Docker stacks with a quick look at the best practices for scaling or restacking an application deployed as a Docker stack.

Best practices for scaling a stack application

As with most things Docker, there are a few different ways to accomplish desired states for your applications. When you are using Docker stacks, you should always use the same method for updating the application as you did for deploying it. Make any desired state changes in the stack compose file, and then run the exact same command you used to deploy the stack. This allows you to use standard source-code-control features to properly handle your compose file, such as tracking and reviewing changes. And, it allows Docker to do the right things for orchestrating your application. If you need to scale a service up or down within your application, you should update the replicas key in the stack compose file and then run the deploy command again. In our example, we have two replicas for our vote service. If the demands for voting skyrocketed, we can easily scale our application by changing the replica value from 2 to, say, 16 by editing the `docker-stack.yml` file, then issuing the same command we originally used to deploy the application:

```
# After updating the docker-stack.yml file, scale the app using the same
deploy command
docker stack deploy -c docker-stack.yml voteapp
```

Now, when we check the services, we can see we are scaling our app:

```
earl@ubuntu-node01:~$ docker stack services voteapp
ID                  NAME                MODE         REPLICAS   IMAGE                                              PORTS
9t7dqhu4u5ym        voteapp_db          replicated   1/1        postgres:9.4
g1i27crjeohg        voteapp_worker      replicated   1/1        dockersamples/examplevotingapp_worker:latest
gfxlshizpnpc        voteapp_redis       replicated   1/1        redis:alpine                                       *:30001->6379/tcp
kf9t3iu27064        voteapp_result      replicated   1/1        dockersamples/examplevotingapp_result:before       *:5001->80/tcp
rfrimdtt7ti8        voteapp_vote        replicated   16/16      dockersamples/examplevotingapp_vote:before          *:5000->80/tcp
xko2kjse9gkf        voteapp_visualizer  replicated   1/1        dockersamples/visualizer:stable                    *:8080->8080/tcp
earl@ubuntu-node01:~$
```

There you have it, an easy-to-use, easy-to-understand, and very, very powerful Docker application orchestration!

References

Check out the following links for more information:

- The compose file reference: https://docs.docker.com/compose/compose-file/
- Some compose file examples: https://github.com/play-with-docker/stacks
- Docker sample images on Docker hub: https://hub.docker.com/u/dockersamples/

- Official redis image tags found on Docker hub: `https://hub.docker.com/r/library/redis/tags/`
- A great article about using the Docker daemon socket: `https://medium.com/lucjuggery/about-var-run-docker-sock-3bfd276e12fd`
- The stack deploy command reference: `https://docs.docker.com/engine/reference/commandline/stack_deploy/`
- The stack ps command reference: `https://docs.docker.com/engine/reference/commandline/stack_ps/`
- The stack services command reference: `https://docs.docker.com/engine/reference/commandline/stack_services/`

Summary

Now you know a lot about Docker stacks. You can easily create application definitions with a compose file and then deploy those applications using the stack deploy command. You can explore the details of your deployed stacks with the ls, ps, and services commands. You can scale your applications with easy modifications to your compose file and by executing the same command used to deploy your app. Finally, you can remove an application that has reached the end of its life with the stack rm command. With great power comes great responsibility, so be very careful with that remove command. You have enough information to create and orchestrate world-class enterprise-grade applications now, so get busy! However, if you would like to learn how to use Docker with Jenkins, you'll be pleased to know that that's the topic of `Chapter 8`, *Docker and Jenkins*, so turn the page and start reading!

8
Docker and Jenkins

In this chapter, we will learn how to leverage Jenkins to build our Docker images and deploy our Docker containers. Next, we will learn how to deploy our Jenkins server as a Docker container. We will follow that by learning how to build Docker images within the Dockerized Jenkins server. This is what is often called Docker in Docker. Finally, we will see how to utilize Docker containers as Jenkins build agents, allowing every build to be run in a pristine, ephemeral Docker container. Of course, we will show how to build Docker images, test applications, and push tested images to a Docker registry, all within our Dockerized Jenkins build agents. This will provide you will all the tools you will need to set up your CI/CD systems.

> *If all the containers in the world were laid end to end, they would go around the earth more than twice.*

> — https://www.bigboxcontainers.co.za/

In this chapter, we will cover the following topics:

- Using Jenkins to build Docker images
- Setting up a Dockerized Jenkins server
- Building Docker images inside a Dockerized Jenkins server
- Using Docker containers for your Jenkins build nodes
- Building, testing, and pushing Docker images inside Dockerized build nodes

Technical requirements

You will be pulling Docker images from Docker's public repo, and installing the Jenkins server software, so basic internet access is required to execute the examples within this chapter. Note also that these examples have higher system requirements than those presented in previous chapters. The server used in this chapter's examples has 8 GB ram, 2 CPUs, and 20 GB of HDD.

The code files of this chapter can be found on GitHub:

```
https://github.com/PacktPublishing/Docker-Quick-Start-Guide/tree/master/
Chapter08
```

Check out the following video to see the code in action:
```
http://bit.ly/2AyRz7k
```

Using Jenkins to build Docker images

You probably already know that Jenkins is a widely-used tool for continuous integration/continuous delivery (CI/CD) systems. Virtually every company, both large and small, is using it in some capacity. It is extremely effective, and highly configurable, especially with the variety of plugins that can be used with it. So, it is very natural to expand its use to create Docker images. This first step in using Jenkins with Docker is pretty easy to accomplish. If you have an existing Jenkins server in use today, all you need to do to use it to build Docker images is to install Docker on the Jenkins server. You use the exact same installation techniques that we saw and used in Chapter 1, *Setting up a Docker Development Environment*. Based on the OS of the system that is running your Jenkins server, you follow the install steps you learned in Chapter 1, *Setting up a Docker Development Environment*; when you are done, you can use Jenkins to build Docker images.

If you don't already have a Jenkins server up and running, you can follow the guide found in the *Installing Jenkins* web page link in the following *References* section and install Jenkins on whatever OS you're using. As an example, we will be using the information from that page to set up a Jenkins server on an Ubuntu system. Start by opening a terminal window. Now get the apt-key for Jenkins packages. Next, you will add the Debian Jenkins source to the apt sources list. Next, you will update the packages on the system, and finally, you will install Jenkins using apt-get. The commands look like the following:

```
# If Java has not yet been installed, install it now
sudo apt install openjdk-8-jre-headless

# Install Jenkins on an Ubuntu system
wget -q -O - https://pkg.jenkins.io/debian/jenkins.io.key | sudo apt-key
add -
sudo sh -c 'echo deb http://pkg.jenkins.io/debian-stable binary/ >
/etc/apt/sources.list.d/jenkins.list'
sudo apt-get update
sudo apt-get install jenkins
```

Running these commands on my system looks like the following:

```
earl@ubuntu-jenkins:~$ wget -q -O - https://pkg.jenkins.io/debian/jenkins.io.key | sudo apt-key add -
OK
earl@ubuntu-jenkins:~$ sudo sh -c 'echo deb http://pkg.jenkins.io/debian-stable binary/ > /etc/apt/sources.list.d/jenkins.list'
earl@ubuntu-jenkins:~$ sudo apt-get update
Ign:1 http://pkg.jenkins.io/debian-stable binary/ InRelease
Hit:2 http://security.ubuntu.com/ubuntu bionic-security InRelease
Hit:3 http://us.archive.ubuntu.com/ubuntu bionic InRelease
Hit:4 https://download.docker.com/linux/ubuntu bionic InRelease
Get:5 http://pkg.jenkins.io/debian-stable binary/ Release [2,042 B]
Hit:6 http://us.archive.ubuntu.com/ubuntu bionic-updates InRelease
Get:7 http://pkg.jenkins.io/debian-stable binary/ Release.gpg [181 B]
Hit:8 http://us.archive.ubuntu.com/ubuntu bionic-backports InRelease
Get:9 http://pkg.jenkins.io/debian-stable binary/ Packages [13.6 kB]
Fetched 15.8 kB in 1s (27.3 kB/s)
Reading package lists... Done
earl@ubuntu-jenkins:~$ sudo apt-get install jenkins
Reading package lists... Done
Building dependency tree
Reading state information... Done
The following additional packages will be installed:
  daemon
The following NEW packages will be installed:
  daemon jenkins
0 upgraded, 2 newly installed, 0 to remove and 372 not upgraded.
Need to get 75.6 MB of archives.
After this operation, 76.1 MB of additional disk space will be used.
Do you want to continue? [Y/n]
```

When the install completes, you will want to open your browser and browse to port `8080` on the system to finish the setup and configuration of your Jenkins system. This will include entering the admin password and then deciding which plugins to install as part of the initial deployment of your Jenkins server. I recommend using the set recommended by Jenkins as it is a great starting point:

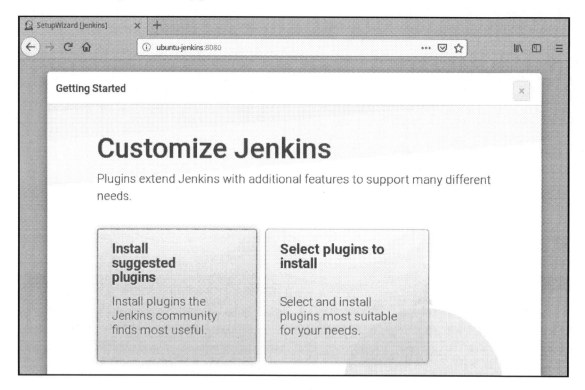

Now that you have a Jenkins server, you can begin creating jobs for it to execute to confirm that it is working as desired. Let's start out with a trivial Hello world! job to confirm that Jenkins is working. Log into your Jenkins server and click on the **New Item** link. In the new item page, enter the name for our job. I'm using `hello-test`. Select the type of job that we want to create as **pipeline**. Next, click the **OK** button near the bottom left of the page. This will take you to the configuration screen for our new job. This one is going to be very simple. We are going to create a pipeline script, so scroll down until you see the Pipeline script input box, and enter the following script (note that the pipeline script is written in groovy, which uses the Java (and C) form of comments):

```
// Our hello world pipeline script, named "hello-test"
node {
    stage('Say Hello') {
```

```
        echo 'Hello Docker Quick Start Guide Readers!'
    }
}
```

That's all for now, so click on the **Save** button to save the updated configuration of our Jenkins job. Once the configuration has been saved, let's test the job by clicking on the **Build now** link. If everything is functioning as expected, we should see the job complete successfully. It will look something like the following:

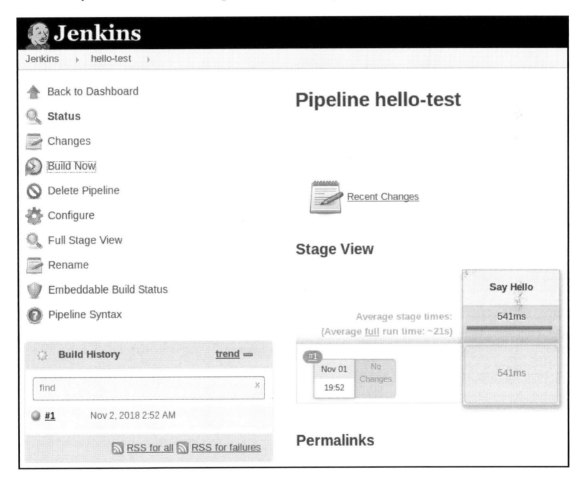

Now let's create another job. Click the link to go back to the dashboard and then click the **New Item** link again. This time, let's name the job `hello-docker-test`. Again, select the pipeline for the type of job you want to create and then click the **OK** button. Again, scroll down to the Pipeline script input and enter the following:

```
// Our Docker hello world pipeline script, named "hello-docker-test"
node {
    stage('Hello via Alpine') {
        docker.image('alpine:latest').inside {
            sh 'echo Hello DQS Readers - from inside an alpine container!'
        }
    }
}
```

Click on the **Save** button to save the configuration for the new job, and then click the **Build Now** link to launch the Jenkins job. The following is what it might look like this time:

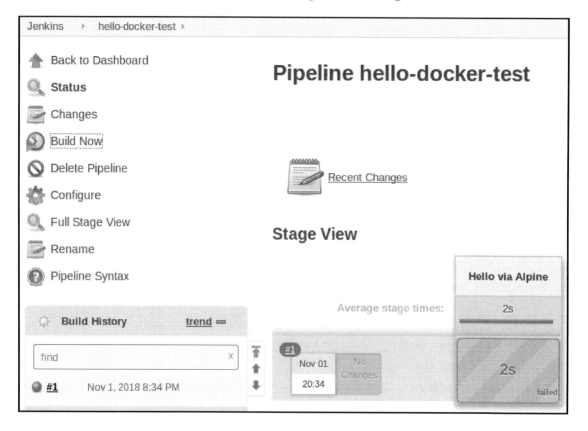

What happened this time? This one didn't complete successfully. Well, obviously it failed because we don't have Docker installed on our Jenkins server yet. So let's go ahead and follow the instructions found in Chapter 1, *Setting up a Docker Development Environment*, for installing Docker, and install it on our Jenkins server. Once you have it installed, there is one additional step you will want to do, which is to add the Jenkins user to the Docker group. The following is the command:

```
# Add the jenkins user to the docker group
sudo usermod -aG docker jenkins
# Then restart the jenkins service
sudo service jenkins restart
```

It is very much like the command we used to add the current user of our Docker server to the docker group so that it was unnecessary to use sudo for Docker commands. OK, now let's go back to our Jenkins server UI and to our hello-docker-test job and click the **Build now** button again.

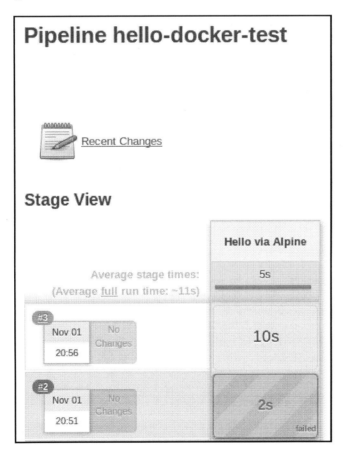

Congratulations! You have a shiny, new Jenkins server, properly configured to build (test, push, and deploy) Docker images. Well done. Still, while this is a great accomplishment, it was kind of a lot of work. Don't you wish there was an easier way to set up a new Jenkins server? So, you know how you already have a nice set of servers running Docker? Do you think you can use that environment to stand up your Jenkins server in an easier way? You betcha! Let's take a look.

References

The following is the web page to install Jenkins: `https://jenkins.io/doc/book/installing/`.

Setting up a Dockerized Jenkins server

You have just seen how much work it is to set up a new Jenkins server. While it is not a Herculean effort, there are at least five steps you have to do before you can pick your plugins and log in to get to work. And in the spirit of the game show *Name That Tune*, I can deploy a Jenkins server in three steps, and the first two are just to allow our Jenkins data to persist beyond the life of the Docker container that hosts the Jenkins server. Assuming you have a Docker host set up-and-running as per the instructions in Chapter 1, *Setting up a Docker Development Environment*, we want to create a location for the Jenkins server to store its data. We will create a folder and assign ownership to it. It will look like the following:

```
# Setup volume location to store Jenkins configuration
mkdir $HOME/jenkins_home
chown 1000 $HOME/jenkins_home
```

The owner `1000` is the user ID that will be used for the jenkins user inside the Docker container.

The third step is to deploy our container. Before I show you the command, let me talk a little about which container image to use. I am including a link for searching on the Docker hub for Jenkins images. If you use that link or search on your own, you will see that there are a lot of options to choose from. Initially, you might think about using the official Jenkins image. However, if you browse to that repo, you will find what I feel is kind of odd, which is that the official image is deprecated. It has stopped being updated past version LTS 2.60.x:

DEPRECATION NOTICE

This image has been deprecated in favor of the `jenkins/jenkins:lts` image provided and maintained by Jenkins Community as part of project's release process. The images found here will receive no further updates after LTS 2.60.x. Please adjust your usage accordingly.

Supported tags and respective `Dockerfile` links

* `latest`, `2.60.3` (*Dockerfile*)
* `alpine`, `2.60.3-alpine` (*Dockerfile*)

It recommends using the image found in the **jenkins/jenkins:lts** Jenkins repo, which at the time of writing is version 2.149.x. This is the image we will use in the following example. The following is the command we are going to use to deploy our Jenkins server container:

```
# Deploy a Jenkins server that is configured to build Docker images
docker container run -d -p 8080:8080 -p 50000:50000 \
-v $HOME/jenkins_home:/var/jenkins_home \
--name jenkins --rm jenkins/jenkins:lts
```

Taking a closer look at this command, we see that we are launching the container as a daemon (non-interactively). We see that we are opening two ports on the host, which are mapped to the same port numbers on the container, specifically `8080` and `50000`. Next, we see that we are using a volume, and it is mapping to the folder we created earlier. This is where Jenkins will store its data, such as the jobs we create and the status of their execution. Then you will notice we are nameing the container `jenkins`. After that, we tell Docker to remove the container when it exits using the `--rm` flag. Finally, we tell Docker what image we want to run.

When you run this container, giving it a minute or two to start up and browse to port `8080` on the Docker host, you will see the same prompt for a password that you see when you deploy Jenkins as a standalone application. That will be followed by the create-the-first-user screen and the default-plugin-configuration screen. Go ahead and give it a try.

Since we have created a volume for the Jenkins data (written to `/var/jenkins_home`), our Jenkins configuration data is being saved to the host and will live beyond the life of the container itself. Of course, you can use a storage driver and have this data somewhere more permanent than the Docker host, but you get the idea, right?

The only problem is that neither the official Jenkins image nor the `jenkins/jenkins` image supports creating jobs that will build a Docker image. And since this book is all about Docker, we need to do something more than just run our Jenkins server using the aforementioned images. Don't worry, I have a plan for that… Keep reading.

References

- Docker hub search for Jenkins images: `https://hub.docker.com/search/? isAutomated=0isOfficial=0page=1pullCount=0q=jenkinsstarCount=0`
- Official Jenkins image repo: `https://hub.docker.com/_/jenkins/`
- Jenkins/jenkins repo: `https://hub.docker.com/r/jenkins/jenkins/`

Building Docker images inside of a Dockerized Jenkins server

Alright. Now you know how to deploy Jenkins as a Docker container, but we really want to be able to use Jenkins to build Docker images, as we did in the standalone deployment of Jenkins. To do that, we could deploy the same Jenkins image, and exec into it and install Docker and could probably get it to work, but we don't need to go to that much trouble. We're not the first pioneers to go down this road. There are several Docker images that have been created to do just what we are looking to do. One such image is `h1kkan/jenkins-docker:lts`. You can read about it by following the link in the following *References* section, but for now just know that it is an image that has been set up as a Jenkins server, and has Docker already installed in it. In fact, it also has Ansible and the AWSCLI pre-installed so you can do more than just build Docker images using it.

To begin, we will create a location on the Docker host to mount a Docker volume to store and preserve the Jenkins configuration. If you are using the same Docker host as you used in the previous section, you should already have created your folder and assigned ownership of it to ID 1000. If not, the following are the commands you use to do so:

```
# Setup volume location to store Jenkins configuration
mkdir $HOME/jenkins_home
chown 1000 $HOME/jenkins_home
```

Also, if you haven't done so already, you can use the `docker container stop jenkins` command to stop (and remove) the Jenkins container that we created in the previous section to clear the way for our new and improved Jenkins server. When you are ready to create the new container, you can use these commands:

```
# Deploy a Jenkins server that is configured to build Docker images
docker container run -d -p 8080:8080 -p 50000:50000 \
-v $HOME/jenkins_home:/var/jenkins_home \
-v /var/run/docker.sock:/var/run/docker.sock \
--name jenkins --rm h1kkan/jenkins-docker:lts
```

```
# Start the Docker service in the Jenkins docker container
docker container exec -it -u root jenkins service docker start
```

You will have noticed a couple of differences in this code block. The first is the use of a second volume. This is a well-known trick, of sorts, that allows a container to issue Docker commands to its host. This essentially allows what is known as Docker-in-Docker. The next difference is an extra Docker command that will start the Docker service inside the running container. Because each container starts up with a single process, having both a Jenkins server process and a Docker daemon running requires this extra step.

Once the Docker service has started within the Jenkins container, you are all set to create new Jenkins jobs that use and build Docker images. You can test it out yourself by recreating the second example above, hello-docker-test, in your new Jenkins server. And since we are using the Docker volume mounted on the host at $HOME/jenkins_home to store our Jenkins data, this should be the last time you need to create this job.

This is all working wonderfully, but you may recall from Chapter 7, *Docker Stacks*, that we have a better way to deploy apps than by using the docker container run command, namely using Docker stacks. So would you like to see our example re-imagined as a Docker stack? Me too! OK then, let's do it.

First off, use the container stop command to stop your current Jenkins container. It will leave behind the jenkins_home folder with our Jenkins server's data, but if for some reason you skipped ahead to this part of the chapter and haven't created that yet, the following are the commands to use:

```
# Setup volume location to store Jenkins configuration
mkdir $HOME/jenkins_home
chown 1000 $HOME/jenkins_home
```

Again, if you did those two commands for one of the previous examples, and you are using the same Docker host, you don't have to do that again because the folder already exists and has the right ownership.

Next, you need to create a compose file for our Jenkins stack. I called mine jenkins-stack.yml and entered the following YML code into it:

```
# jenkins-stack.yml
version: "3"
services:
  jenkins:
    image: h1kkan/jenkins-docker:lts
    ports:
      - 8080:8080
      - 50000:50000
```

```
    volumes:
      - $HOME/jenkins_home:/var/jenkins_home
      - /var/run/docker.sock:/var/run/docker.sock
    deploy:
      replicas: 1
      restart_policy:
        condition: on-failure
    placement:
      constraints: [node.role == manager]

  registry:
    image: registry
    ports:
      - 5000:5000
deploy:
  replicas: 1
  restart_policy:
    condition: on-failure
```

You will notice that we are creating two services; one is our Jenkins server, and the other is a Docker registry. We will use the registry service in an upcoming example, so keep that in your back pocket for now. Looking at the Jenkins service description, there is nothing we did not see already in Chapter 7, *Docker Stacks*, when we learned about Docker stacks. You will notice our two port mappings and the two volumes that were used in the last example. We are confining the single Jenkins replica to our manager node.

Remember that to use Docker stacks we have to be running in swarm mode, so if you have not done so already, create your swarm with the docker swarm init command that we learned in Chapter 5, *Docker Swarm*.

 Understand that if your swarm has more than one manager node, you will need to further confine the Jenkins replica to just the single manager that has your jenkins_home volume mount point. This can be accomplished with a combination of roles and labels. Alternatively, you can use a storage driver and mount a volume that can be shared among swarm managers. For simplicity, we are assuming a single manager node for our example.

Now use the stack deploy command to set up the Jenkins application. The following is an example of the command to use:

```
# Deploy our Jenkins application via a Docker stack
docker stack deploy -c jenkins-stack.yml jenkins
```

Once the stack is deployed and the services up and running, you can browse to any node in your swarm, on port 8080, and get to your Jenkins server. What's more, if you are reusing the `jenkins_home` folder from our previous example, you will not have to supply the admin password, create a new user, and select your plugins because all of the data related to those tasks was stored in the `jenkins_home` folder and is reused now by your stack-based Jenkins service. One more interesting note is that you do not have to start the Docker service when you use this image in a stack application. Bonus!

OK, we now have a sweet stack-based Jenkins service that is capable of using and building Docker images. Everything seems right with the World. But there is one thing that could make this better. And by better, I mean more Docker-y: instead of using the normal Jenkins agents for our build jobs, what if we wanted to spin up a new, pristine Docker container to use for each execution of our Jenkins jobs? This would ensure that every build was built from scratch in a clean, consistent environment. Plus, it really takes the Docker inception level up a notch, so I like it a lot. If you want to see how it's done, keep reading.

References

- H1kkan/jenkins-docker repo: `https://hub.docker.com/r/h1kkan/jenkins-docker/`

Using Docker containers for your Jenkins build nodes

To use Docker containers for the Jenkins build agents, you need to do a few things to your Jenkins configuration:

- Build a new Docker image that can act as a Jenkins build agent, and is capable of building Docker images (of course)
- Push the new image to a Docker registry
- Turn off the default Jenkins build agents
- Install the Docker plugin for Jenkins
- Configure a new cloud to enable Dockerized build agents

Building the Docker image

Let's get started. The first thing we want to do is build our specialized Docker image that can be used for our Jenkins agents. To do this, we are going to use the skills we learned in Chapter 3, *Creating Docker Images*, to create Docker images. Start by creating a new folder on your development system, and then change your working directory to that folder. I named mine jenkins-agent:

```
# Make a new folder to use for the build context of your new Docker image,
and cd into it
mkdir jenkins-agent
cd jenkins-agent
```

Now create a new file, named Dockerfile, using your favorite editor, enter the following code into it, and then save it:

```
# jenkins-agent Dockerfile
FROM h1kkan/jenkins-docker:lts-alpine
USER root
ARG user=jenkins

ENV HOME /home/${user}
ARG VERSION=3.26
ARG AGENT_WORKDIR=/home/${user}/agent

RUN apk add --update --no-cache curl bash git openssh-client openssl procps
\
 && curl --create-dirs -sSLo /usr/share/jenkins/slave.jar
https://repo.jenkins-ci.org/public/org/jenkins-ci/main/remoting/${VERSION}/
remoting-${VERSION}.jar \
 && chmod 755 /usr/share/jenkins \
 && chmod 644 /usr/share/jenkins/slave.jar \
 && apk del curl

ENV AGENT_WORKDIR=${AGENT_WORKDIR}
RUN mkdir -p /home/${user}/.jenkins && mkdir -p ${AGENT_WORKDIR}
USER ${user}

VOLUME /home/${user}/.jenkins
VOLUME ${AGENT_WORKDIR}
WORKDIR /home/${user}
```

Here is what our new Dockerfile is doing: in our FROM instruction, we are using the same Docker image that we used in our Docker-in-Docker example above so that we have a base image that will allow us to build Docker images. Next, we use the USER command to set the current user to root. Next, we create an ARG named user and set it to a value of jenkins. After that, we set an environment variable named HOME that has a value for the Jenkins user's home folder. Then, we set two more ARGs, one for the version and one for the Jenkins agent's working directory. The next one is where the magic happens. We are using a RUN command to set up and curl the Jenkins slave.jar file. This is the bit that is required to run as a Jenkins agent. We also set some permissions on the folder and file, and then clean up a bit by deleting curl. After that, we set another environment variable, this one for AGENT_WORKDIR. Next up, we create a couple of folders in the container. Then, we use the USER instruction again, this time setting the current user to our Jenkins user. We round out the Dockerfile by creating a couple of VOLUME instances and, finally, we set the current working directory to the home directory for our Jenkins user. Phew! That seems like a lot, but really it's not so bad, and all you have to do copy and paste the preceding code into your Dockerfile and save it.

Now that we have our Dockerfile ready to use, it might be a good time to create a git repo and save your code to it. Once you are satisfied that your project has been properly set up with git, we can build our new Docker image. The following is the command you will use for that:

```
# Build our new Jenkins agent image
docker image build -t jenkins-agent:latest .
```

It should build successfully and create a locally-cached image tagged as jenkins-agent:latest.

Pushing the new image to a Docker registry

Next, we need to push our new image to a Docker registry. Of course, we could push it to our repo within hub.docker.com, but since we have an application stack that just so happens to have deployed a Docker registry, why don't we utilize it for our Jenkins agent image? First, we need to tag our new image with the registry. Your tag command will differ from mine based on the domain name of your Docker swarm, but for my example, the following is what my tag command looks like:

```
# Tag the image with our swarm service registry
docker image tag jenkins-agent:latest ubuntu-node01:5000/jenkins-agent:latest
```

Now that the image is tagged locally, we can push it to the registry with the following command; again, your command will be different based on the domain name of your swarm:

```
# Push the Jenkins agent image to the registry
docker image push ubuntu-node01:5000/jenkins-agent:latest
```

All of these commands might utilize a better version scheme than the oversimplified use of the `latest` tag, but you should be able to address that on your own. With our image built, tagged, and pushed to the Docker registry, we are ready to update our Jenkins configuration to use it.

Turning off the default Jenkins build agents

Now we are ready to update our Jenkins configuration to support our Dockerized build agents. The first configuration change we are going to make is to turn off the default build agents. To do this, log into your Jenkins server, and click the **Manage Jenkins** menu link. This will take you to a variety of configuration groups you can manage, such as system, plugins, and CLI settings. For now, we will need to go to the **Configure System** management group:

Once you are in the **Configure System** management group, you are going to change the value for # **of executors** to 0. It should look something like the following:

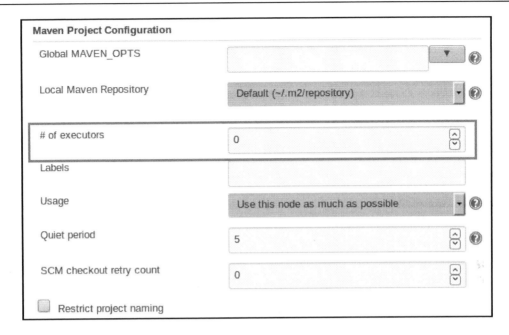

When you have changed the **# of executors** value to 0, you can go ahead and save the settings by clicking the **Save** button in the lower-left part of the screen. At this point, with this change in place, your Jenkins server will not be able to run any jobs because there are no Jenkins agents configured to run them. So let's move on quickly to the next step, which is to install the Docker plugin.

Installing the Docker plugin for Jenkins

Now we need to install the Docker plugin for Jenkins. You accomplish this as you would other plugin installations. Click on the **Manage Jenkins** menu link, and from the list of configuration groups, click the link for the **Manage Plugins** group:

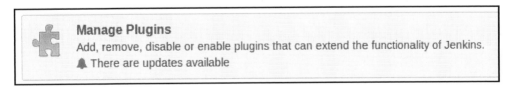

Once you are in the **Manage Plugins** configuration group, select the tab for **Available** plugins, and then in the filter box, type `docker` to narrow down the list of available plugins to those related to Docker:

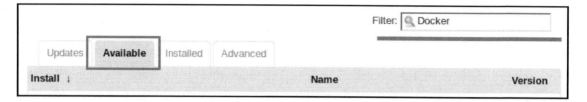

Even with a filtered list, there are still a lot of plugins to choose from. Find and check the box for the **Docker** plugin. It looks like the following:

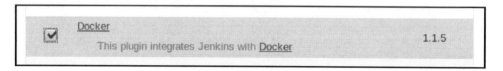

With the **Docker** plugin checkbox checked, scroll down and click the **Install without restart** button. This will download and install the plugin for you, and then enable it as soon as Jenkins restarts. On the install screen, you have the option to execute a restart as soon as the plugin is installed. To do this, check the **Restart Jenkins when installation is complete and no jobs are running** checkbox:

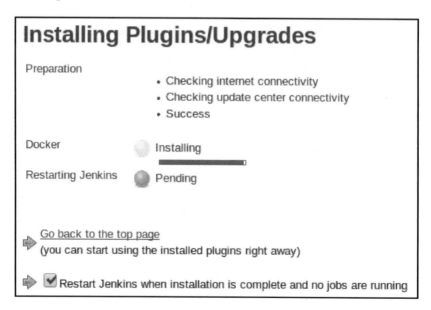

Since we set the **# of executors** to 0 a few minutes ago, there will not be any jobs running now, so as soon as the plugin is installed, Jenkins will restart. As soon as Jenkins comes back online, the plugin will be installed. We need to log back in to Jenkins and set up our Cloud.

Creating a new Cloud to enable our Dockerized build agents

Now we will tell Jenkins to use our custom Docker image to run containers as Jenkins build agents. Once more, click on the **Manage Jenkins** menu link. From the list of configuration groups, you will again click the link for the **Configure System** group. You will find the **Cloud** configuration near the bottom of the configuration options. Click on the **Add a new cloud** dropdown and select Docker:

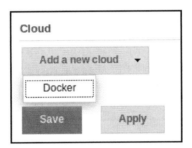

The screen will update and you will have two new configuration groups: **Docker Cloud details...** and **Docker Agent templates...**:

Let's take care of the Docker Cloud details first. Click on that button now. You can leave the **Name** value as the default for `docker`. In the Docker Host URI field, enter `unix:///var/run/docker.sock`. You can find this value by clicking the question mark help icon and copying and pasting it into the input field. Next, click the **Test Connection** button and you should see a version line show up, similar to the one you will see in the following screenshot. Make note of the API Version number as you will need it for the **Advanced...** setup. Click the **Advanced...** button and enter the API Version number in the **Docker API Version** field. You need to check the **Enabled** checkbox to enable this feature, so be sure to do so. Finally, you may want to change the number of containers that the system can run concurrently. The default is 100. For my example, I reduced the value to 10. When you are done, your configuration should look something like the following:

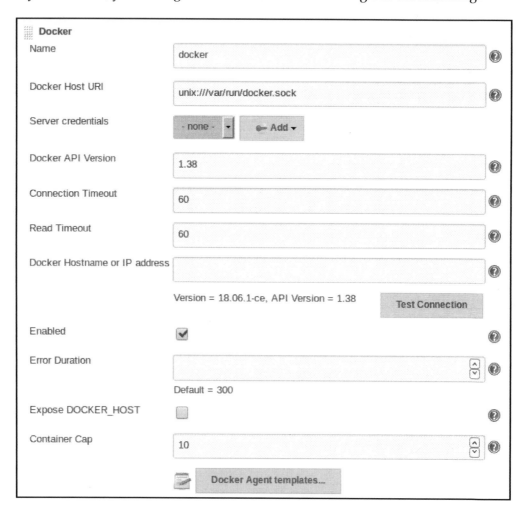

Next, click the **Docker Agent templates...** button and then click the **Add Docker template** button that appears so that we can to configure the Jenkins agent settings. Here, you will want to click the agent's **Enabled** checkbox to enable our new agent template. You can give a name to use as the prefix for the containers that are run by Jenkins as the build agents, or you can leave the name blank and the `docker` prefix will be used. Next, enter the repository and the name tag for the image you want to use for the build agent containers. We created our custom image, tagged it, and pushed it to our Jenkins stack application repo using the `ubuntu-node01:5000/jenkins-agent:latest` image name, so enter that value into the Docker Image field. Set the **Instance Capacity** value to 1, and the **Remote File System Root** value to `/home/jenkins/agent`. Make sure the **Usage** value is set to `Use this node as much as possible`, and use the `Attach Docker container` value for the **Connect method**. Set the User to `root`. Change the **Pull strategy** value to `Pull once and update latest`:

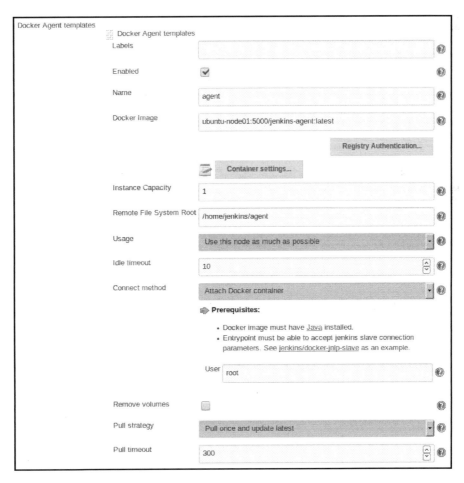

Finally, we need to configure some **Container settings...**, so click to expand that section. The value we need to enter here is the command we want to use when the container is run. The value you need in the **Docker Command** field is `java -jar /usr/share/jenkins/slave.jar`. The value you need in the **Volumes** field is `/var/run/docker.sock:/var/run/docker.sock:`

And lastly, check the checkbox for **Allocate a pseudo-TTY**:

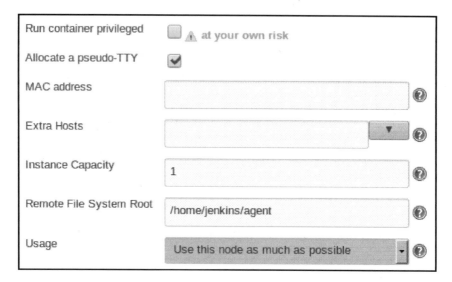

Scroll down to the bottom of the configuration screen and click the **Save** button to save all of the **Cloud** settings. That was some serious configuration Kung Fu—great job! However, just in case you want a quick reference for all of the values entered, here are all of the custom (or non-default) values entered to configure the Docker Cloud in our example:

Field name	Value used
Docker Host URI	`unix:///var/run/docker.sock`
Docker API Version	`1.38` (match the version shown in the connection test)
Docker Cloud Enabled	Checked
Container Cap	`10`
Docker Agent Enabled	Checked
Docker Agent Template Name	`agent`
Docker Image	`ubuntu-node01:5000/jenkins-agent:latest`
Instance Capacity	`1`
Remote File System Root	`/home/jenkins/agent`
Usage	`Use this node as much as possible`
Connection Method	`Attach Docker container`
User	`root`
Pull Strategy	`Pull once and update latest`
Docker Command	`java -jar /usr/share/jenkins/slave.jar`
Volumes	`/var/run/docker.sock:/var/run/docker.sock`
Allocate a pseudo-TTY	Checked

Now that everything is configured, let's give our newly-defined Jenkins agents a test.

Testing our new build agents

Head back to the Jenkins dashboard and click on the **Schedule a Build** button for our `hello-docker-test` job. This will start a new build for our job, which in turn will create a new Dockerized build agent. It uses the configuration we set to execute a `docker container run` command to run a new container based on the image we specified. Initially, the executor will be offline as the container spins up:

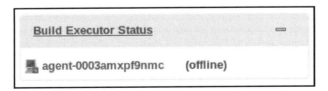

Notice that the executor name has the **agent** prefix that we specified. Once the container is running, the Jenkins job will be initiated within it, essentially using the `docker container exec` command. When the Jenkins job has started, the normal job-progress graphic will display, and the executor will no longer show as offline. The status will then look something like this:

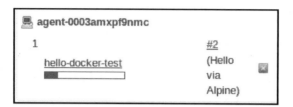

If you click on the progress bar of the executing job, you can view the job's console output, and after a short while the job will show the finished: **SUCCESS** status, like the following:

```
Console Output

Started by user Earl Waud
Running in Durability level: MAX_SURVIVABILITY
[Pipeline] node
Running on agent-0003amxpf9nmc on docker in /home/jenkins/agent/workspace/hello-docker-test
[Pipeline] {
[Pipeline] stage
[Pipeline] { (Hello via Alpine)
[Pipeline] sh
[hello-docker-test] Running shell script
+ docker inspect -f . alpine:latest

[Pipeline] withDockerContainer
agent-0003amxpf9nmc on docker seems to be running inside container
d09fd6c427a492d4d16dfc3e5f8e321576be020b1e396924c6eee823b9ce498b
$ docker run -t -d -u 0:0 -w /home/jenkins/agent/workspace/hello-docker-test --volumes-from
d09fd6c427a492d4d16dfc3e5f8e321576be020b1e396924c6eee823b9ce498b -e ******** -e ******** -e ******** -e
******** -e ******** -e ******** -e ******** -e ******** -e ******** -e ******** -e ******** -e ******** -e
******** -e ******** -e ******** -e ******** -e ******** -e ******** -e ******** -e ******** -e ******** -e
******** -e ******** -e ******** alpine:latest cat
$ docker top 02d4a37692271cf5334ea9d60da0fb141b4face61034490ecbf1da29f847b1a1 -eo pid,comm
[Pipeline] {
[Pipeline] sh
[hello-docker-test] Running shell script
+ echo Hello DQS Readers - from inside an alpine 'container!'
Hello DQS Readers - from inside an alpine container!
[Pipeline] }
$ docker stop --time=1 02d4a37692271cf5334ea9d60da0fb141b4face61034490ecbf1da29f847b1a1
$ docker rm -f 02d4a37692271cf5334ea9d60da0fb141b4face61034490ecbf1da29f847b1a1
[Pipeline] // withDockerContainer
[Pipeline] }
[Pipeline] // stage
[Pipeline] }
[Pipeline] // node
[Pipeline] End of Pipeline
Finished: SUCCESS
```

A job well done! Let's examine one last example Jenkins job to show a pipeline script that has more stages, and represents a real-world example of a Docker job. Are you ready? Read on.

Building, testing, and pushing Docker images inside Dockerized build nodes

To wrap up this chapter on Docker and Jenkins, let's walk through the steps of creating a template for a real-world Dockerized node application. The following is what we will do:

Prepare our application:

- Create a new repo on GitHub
- Clone the repo to our development workstation
- Create our application files
- Push our application files up to GitHub

Create and test the Jenkins job that will build our Dockerized node application:

- Create a new Jenkins job that utilizes the GitHub repo
- Test our Jenkins job that will pull the repo, build the app, test it, and publish the image
- Celebrate our success!

Let's begin by preparing our application.

The first thing we want to do is create our application repo on GitHub. Browse and log into github.com, go to your repositories page, and click on the **Create New Repo** button. Enter a name for the new repository. For our example, I used dqs-example-app. Enter an appropriate description. You can make your repo public or private. For this example, I am keeping it public for the simplicity of not needing to authenticate to pull the repo later. Check the **Initialize the repository** checkbox so you can immediately clone the empty repo on your workstation. You can select the project type to use when creating the .gitignore file. I selected Node. When you have entered and selected all this, it will look much like the following:

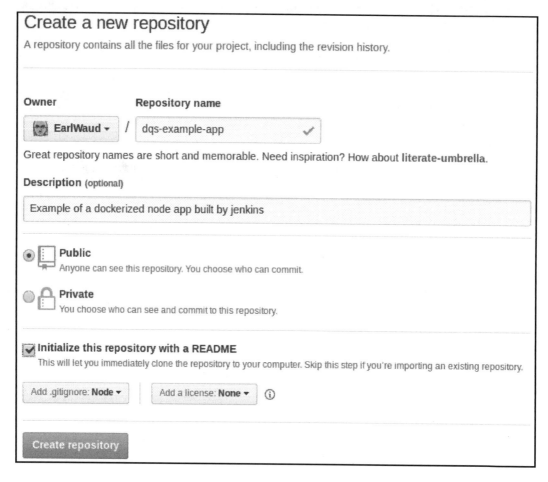

Click on the **Create repository** button to create your new application repo. Now that it is created on GitHub, you will want to clone it to your workstation. Use the **Clone or download** button and then the copy button to copy the repo's URL for the cloning step:

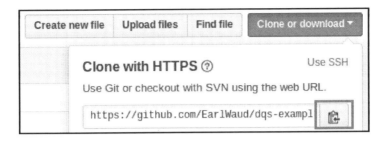

Now, return to your workstation and, in the location where you keep your local repos, clone the new (mostly) empty repo. Then change directory into the new repo's folder. For me, that looked like the following:

```
earl@ubuntu-node01:~$ git clone https://github.com/EarlWaud/dqs-example-app.git
Cloning into 'dqs-example-app'...
remote: Enumerating objects: 4, done.
remote: Counting objects: 100% (4/4), done.
remote: Compressing objects: 100% (4/4), done.
remote: Total 4 (delta 0), reused 0 (delta 0), pack-reused 0
Unpacking objects: 100% (4/4), done.
earl@ubuntu-node01:~$ cd dqs-example-app/
earl@ubuntu-node01:~/dqs-example-app$ █
```

Now we are going to create the application's scaffolding. This will consist of creating a `Dockerfile`, a `Jenkinsfile`, the `main.js` and `test.js` files, and the `package.json` file. Use your favorite editor to create each of these files in your application folder. The following are the contents for the files:

The following are the contents of the `Dockerfile` file:

```
FROM node:10-alpine
COPY . .
RUN npm install
EXPOSE 8000
CMD npm start
```

The following are the contents of the `Jenkinsfile` file:

```
node {
    def app
    stage('Clone repository') {
        /* Clone the repository to our workspace */
        checkout scm
    }
    stage('Build image') {
```

```
        /* Builds the image; synonymous to docker image build on the command
line */
        /* Use a registry name if pushing into docker hub or your company
registry, like this */
        /* app = docker.build("earlwaud/jenkins-example-app") */
        app = docker.build("jenkins-example-app")
    }
    stage('Test image') {
        /* Execute the defined tests */
        app.inside {
            sh 'npm test'
        }
    }
    stage('Push image') {
        /* Now, push the image into the registry */
        /* This would probably be docker hub or your company registry, like
this */
        /* docker.withRegistry('https://registry.hub.docker.com', 'docker-
hub-credentials') */

        /* For this example, We are using our jenkins-stack service registry
*/
        docker.withRegistry('https://ubuntu-node01:5000') {
            app.push("latest")
        }
    }
}
```

The following are the contents of the main.js file:

```
// load the http module
var http = require('http');

// configure our HTTP server
var server = http.createServer(function (request, response) {
    response.writeHead(200, {"Content-Type": "text/plain"});
    response.end("Hello Docker Quick Start\n");
});

// listen on localhost:8000
server.listen(8000);
console.log("Server listening at http://127.0.0.1:8000/");
```

The following are the contents of the package.json file:

```
{
    "name": "dqs-example-app",
    "version": "1.0.0",
```

```
    "description": "A Docker Quick Start Example HTTP server",
    "main": "main.js",
    "scripts": {
        "test": "node test.js",
        "start": "node main.js"
    },
    "repository": {
        "type": "git",
        "url": "https://github.com/earlwaud/dqs-example-app/"
    },
    "keywords": [
        "node",
        "docker",
        "dockerfile",
        "jenkinsfile"
    ],
    "author": "earlwaud@hotmail.com",
    "license": "ISC",
    "devDependencies": { "test": ">=0.6.0" }
}
```

And finally, the following are the contents of the test.js file:

```
var assert = require('assert')

function test() {
    assert.equal(1 + 1, 2);
}

if (module == require.main) require('test').run(test);
```

When you are all done, your repo folder should look something like the following:

```
earl@ubuntu-node01:~/dqs-example-app$ ll
total 40
drwxrwxr-x  3 earl earl 4096 Nov  4 12:24 ./
drwxr-xr-x 20 earl earl 4096 Nov  4 12:19 ../
-rw-rw-r--  1 earl earl   71 Nov  4 12:24 Dockerfile
drwxrwxr-x  8 earl earl 4096 Nov  4 11:56 .git/
-rw-rw-r--  1 earl earl  914 Nov  4 11:56 .gitignore
-rw-rw-r--  1 earl earl 1037 Nov  4 12:06 Jenkinsfile
-rw-rw-r--  1 earl earl  361 Nov  4 11:57 main.js
-rw-rw-r--  1 earl earl  496 Nov  4 12:09 package.json
-rw-rw-r--  1 earl earl   68 Nov  4 11:56 README.md
-rw-rw-r--  1 earl earl  135 Nov  4 12:10 test.js
earl@ubuntu-node01:~/dqs-example-app$ 
```

Now, let's push our work up to the GitHub repo. You will use standard git commands to add the files, commit the files, and then push the files up to the repo. The following are the commands I used:

```
# Initial commit of our application files to the new repo
git add Dockerfile Jenkinsfile main.js package.json test.js
git commit -m "Initial commit"
git push origin master
```

The following is what that looked like for me:

```
earl@ubuntu-node01:~/dqs-example-app$ git add Dockerfile Jenkinsfile main.js package.json test.js
earl@ubuntu-node01:~/dqs-example-app$ git commit -m "Initial commit"
[master 0a0f3ea] Initial commit
 5 files changed, 79 insertions(+)
 create mode 100644 Dockerfile
 create mode 100644 Jenkinsfile
 create mode 100644 main.js
 create mode 100644 package.json
 create mode 100644 test.js
earl@ubuntu-node01:~/dqs-example-app$ git push origin master
Username for 'https://github.com': earlwaud
Password for 'https://earlwaud@github.com':
Counting objects: 7, done.
Compressing objects: 100% (7/7), done.
Writing objects: 100% (7/7), 1.56 KiB | 1.56 MiB/s, done.
Total 7 (delta 0), reused 0 (delta 0)
To https://github.com/EarlWaud/dqs-example-app.git
   aa292b5..0a0f3ea  master -> master
earl@ubuntu-node01:~/dqs-example-app$
```

Now that the initial version of our application has been created and pushed to our GitHub repo, we are ready to create the Jenkins job to pull our repo code, build our application image, test it, and then publish our application's Docker image. Start off by creating a new Jenkins job, by logging into your Jenkins server and clicking on the **New Item** link. Next, enter the name you want to use for the job in the **Enter an item name** input box. I am using dqs-example-app. Select Pipeline for the type of job we are creating, and then click the **OK** button.

You can, and probably should, provide a meaningful description for the build job we are creating. Just enter it into the **Description:** input box at the top of the configuration screen. For our example, I have entered the somewhat terse description Build the dqs-example-app using a pipeline script from SCM. You can probably do a lot better.

We are going to set up the Jenkins job to poll the GitHub repo every five minutes to look for changes to the master branch. There are better options where changes to the repo can trigger the build job without scheduled polling, but for the simplicity of this example, we will just use a poll method. So scroll down to the **Build Triggers** section of the job's configuration and check **Poll SCM**. Then in the schedule, enter a value of H/5 * * * *:

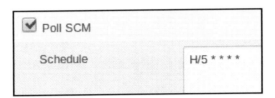

Next, we want to set up our pipeline. Unlike the previous examples, this time we will select the **Pipeline script from SCM** option. We will select Git for our **SCM**, and then enter the Repository URL for our application's repo on GitHub. For this example, that URL is https://github.com/EarlWaud/dqs-example-app.git. Make sure that the **Branches to build** value is set to */master, which is the default value. Your pipeline definition should like a lot like the following:

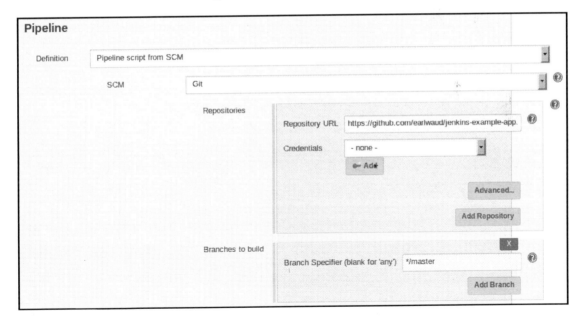

There is one more key setting for the pipeline, and that is the **Script Path**. This is the (path and) filename to the Jenkins script file. In our case, that is literally just `Jenkinsfile` because the name we gave the file is `Jenkinsfile` and it is in the root of our repo. This is what our example's input looks like:

That is all the configuration needed at this time. Everything else is already set up in our source files, and they will be pulled from our application repo. All that's left to do for the configuration is to click the **Save** button. Back at the job's page, we are ready to execute our first build. The newly-created job screen looks like this in our example:

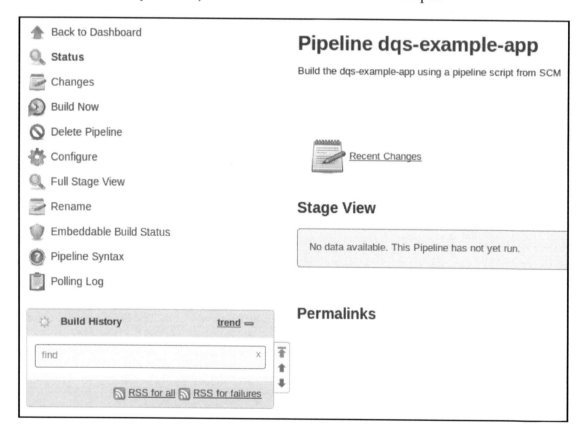

Now, just wait. In five minutes or fewer, the first build of the job will kick off automatically because we have set up polling the repo at five-minute intervals. We will take a look at the console log when the job has finished, but first here is our Jenkins job view after the job completes (successfully, of course!):

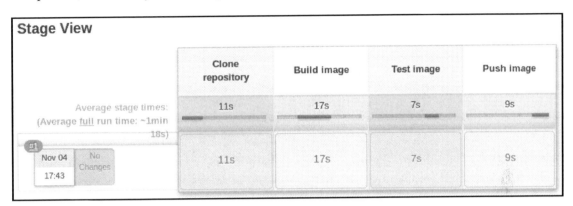

The following is an edited view of the console log output for reference (the full log output can be found in the source bundle):

```
Started by an SCM change
Started by user Earl Waud
Obtained Jenkinsfile from git
https://github.com/EarlWaud/dqs-example-app.git
[Pipeline] node
Running on agent-00042y2g983xq on docker in
/home/jenkins/agent/workspace/dqs-example-app
[Pipeline] { (Clone repository)
Cloning repository https://github.com/EarlWaud/dqs-example-app.git
> git init /home/jenkins/agent/workspace/dqs-example-app # timeout=10
[Pipeline] { (Build image)
+ docker build -t jenkins-example-app .
Successfully built b228cd7c0013
Successfully tagged jenkins-example-app:latest
[Pipeline] { (Test image)
+ docker inspect -f . jenkins-example-app
+ npm test
> node test.js
Passed:1 Failed:0 Errors:0
[Pipeline] { (Push image)
+ docker tag jenkins-example-app ubuntu-node01:5000/jenkins-example-
app:latest
+ docker push ubuntu-node01:5000/jenkins-example-app:latest
Finished: SUCCESS
```

All that is left to do now is celebrate our success:

Seriously, this is a great foundation for creating your own Dockerized applications and building, testing and publishing them using Jenkins. Consider it as a template that you can reuse and build from. You are now ready to utilize Docker with Jenkins in any way you desire.

Summary

Well, here we are, at the end of the chapter. I hope you had as much fun reading this chapter as I had writing it. We had the opportunity to use many of the skills that we learned in the previous chapters. Not only that, there are some really useful Jenkins lessons in this chapter as well. So much so that you could seriously consider skipping any planned Jenkins training or book-reading because pretty much everything you need to know about using Jenkins is right here.

Let's recap: first, we learned how to set up a standalone Jenkins server. We quickly transitioned into deploying a Jenkins server as a Docker container. That's the kind of thing you're reading this book for, right? Then we learned how to build a Docker image in a Dockerized Jenkins server. Next, we found out how to replace the boring Jenkins agents with super-cool Docker containers that can build our Docker image. You might think about this and Docker-in-Docker-in-Docker. Have you seen the movie Inception? Well, you just lived it. Finally, to wrap up the chapter, we created an example dockerized app and the Jenkins job that builds, tests, and publishes that app's image. It's an example that you can use as a template and foundation for the real-world applications you will create in the future.

And, here we are at the end of the book. I'll say it again... I hope you had as much fun reading it as I had writing it. And I hope you learned as much reading it as I did writing it. We covered a lot of Docker information throughout these chapters. We nailed Docker workstation setup in the `Chapter 1`, *Setting up a Dockerized Development Environment,* regardless of the type of OS you prefer. In `Chapter 2`, *Learning Docker Commands,* we learned just about everything there is to know about the Docker command set. In `Chapter 3`, *Creating Docker Images,* we studied the `Dockerfile` instruction set in depth and learned how to create just about any Docker image you could want to build. Chapter 4, *Docker Volumes,* showed us the power and usefulness of Docker volumes. We started putting several of the lessons from the earlier chapters to use when we exercised the features of the almost magical Docker swarm in `Chapter 5`, *Docker Swarm.* Then, in `Chapter 6`, *Docker Networking,* we continued our Docker education, this time learning how Docker has simplified the complex topic of networking for us. And in `Chapter 7`, *Docker Stacks,* we saw more Docker magic and power when we learned about Docker stacks. Finally, in `Chapter 8`, *Docker and Jenkins,* we put all of our learning to use and leveraged Docker with Jenkins to prepare us to create real-world applications.

All that is left is for me to say thanks and wish you success in your Docker journey.

Other Books You May Enjoy

If you enjoyed this book, you may be interested in these other books by Packt:

Docker Cookbook - Second Edition
Jeeva S. Chelladhurai, Ken Cochrane, Et al
ISBN 978-1-78862-686-6

- Install Docker on various platforms
- Work with Docker images and containers
- Container networking and data sharing
- Docker APIs and language bindings
- Various PaaS solutions for Docker
- Implement container orchestration using Docker Swarm and Kubernetes
- Container security
- Docker on various clouds

Containerizing Java EE 8 Apps Using Docker and Kubernetes [Video]
Sebastian Daschner
ISBN: 978-1-78883-338-7

- Package, distribute, and run applications in Docker containers
- Install and configure containerized Java EE application servers
- Deploy enterprise applications as Kubernetes pods, deployments, and services
- Leverage Kubernetes' production-readiness
- Configure containerized and orchestrated applications
- Realize persistence in cluster environments
- Access orchestrated external systems
- Troubleshoot containers and orchestration environments

Leave a review - let other readers know what you think

Please share your thoughts on this book with others by leaving a review on the site that you bought it from. If you purchased the book from Amazon, please leave us an honest review on this book's Amazon page. This is vital so that other potential readers can see and use your unbiased opinion to make purchasing decisions, we can understand what our customers think about our products, and our authors can see your feedback on the title that they have worked with Packt to create. It will only take a few minutes of your time, but is valuable to other potential customers, our authors, and Packt. Thank you!

Index

Made in the USA
San Bernardino, CA
21 June 2019